Edinburgh Review 136

Edinburgh Review
Editor: Alan Gillis
Assistant editor and production: Jennie Renton
Marketing and events: Lynsey May
Additional assistance: Roisin O'Brien and Lisa Parr

Advisory Board: Janice Galloway, Kathleen Jamie, Robert Alan Jamieson, James Loxley, Brian McCabe, Randall Stevenson, Alan Warner

Published by
Edinburgh Review
22a Buccleuch Place
Edinburgh EH8 9LN

edinburghreview@ed.ac.uk
www.edinburgh-review.com

Edinburgh Review 136
ISBN 978-0-9564983-7-3
ISSN 0267-6672

Edinburgh Review
is supported by

ALBA | CHRUTHACHAIL

Contents

No Shouting Out

Hannah McGill

Dorothy Pugh

Dorothy Pugh lives two doors down. For some time now she has been effecting a slow transfer of objects from my house into hers. It started with a recipe book. I was in her kitchen clutching a mug of coffee and this recipe book was on the breakfast bar between us. It was mine, I knew it well, it had a water ripple through the pages and a spine-break at the paella page. *Spanish Countryside Cuisine.* 'Spanish Countryside Cuisine,' I said out loud, thinking that Dorothy would realise and blush and tell me that she'd borrowed it and forgot to say and did I mind and could I advise her please on her paella because she'd tried and tried and the consistency just didn't match mine? But she just did this sleepy smile, touched the book as if it was a nice dog and said, 'Oh my God, ever since Malaga I have just been craving *boquerones en escabeche*.' Then she picked it up and put it on the shelf of her Welsh dresser, next to a dried-flower arrangement that I recognised from the alcove in my spare bedroom. When I went back home and surveyed my house I noticed other things were missing: two hand towels, a boxed Dundee cake, one of the sofa cushions and my husband's golf clubs. I am keeping abreast now and I know that she steals something every time that she comes round. I also think that she has had a set of keys cut, so that she can steal things when I am not there; and that my husband has been helping her with some of the heavier items.

I started keeping a log book. But then Dorothy Pugh stole my fountain pen.

She comes round for coffee, day after day. It's a habit. I imagine that's what she tells people: 'Poor thing two doors down, I do drop in, it's a habit.' I have a strong suspicion (strong enough that I can see it reel by in my mind like a scene from a film) that early in our marriage my husband Had A Word with Dorothy Pugh, and made the suggestion that She Might Pop In On Me. 'You might pop in on her. Old stick, gets tetchy, you know, solo, all hours. Might you pop in? So kind. Busy woman like you.' Each day I wait anxiously for her to arrive: I bite my nails and arrange the items on the table so that it looks as if I have been making a soup. I *have in fact* been making a soup, but it doesn't really look as if I have – or not in a good way. So I put the onion in a nicer position and I hide the OXO cube foil.

I wait anxiously for her to arrive and then once she arrives I wait anxiously for her to leave.

You would not think to look at us that Dorothy would want my things. You might rather expect it to work the other way round. I am a shaggy sort of woman, I have spread outside my clothes, I have not bought new ones, I have allowed my hair to donkey. Dorothy is angular and blonde. She clicks when she walks, and it is something she makes jokes about, ruefully, as if it is a humiliating flaw. I think she does this in order to draw attention to how thin she is. *My bones, see how they stick out, it's so problematic being fragile like me!* Walking behind her on the stairs I wish things upon her and her bones: ARTHRITIS, OSTEOPOROSIS. I walk behind her on the stairs because I follow her in an effort to limit her stealing. 'I'm going to use your bathroom, sweetheart,' she says, and I jump up and follow: I just need to fetch my reading glasses, I say, or set the alarm clock, or see about the cat. Click, click, click go the backs of her knees. I stand breathless on the landing while Dorothy Pugh pees, I listen tight-headed for the tiny whisper of her wiping, but following her doesn't seem to make any difference. Still in her wake there are gone things. As the door shuts behind her latest visit, and the heat fades from her lipstuck coffee cup, I notice the latest gaps. Clean dustless spaces on the mantle where once sat souvenirs. Unfaded square shapes on the wallpaper, missing the pictures that made them. I spider the house, touching where things aren't. How is she doing it. How are you doing it. How is she doing it, Dorothy Pugh.

I made a mistake: I told her that my husband had a very large penis, a penis so large that it was uncomfortable for me to have sex with him especially in certain positions which happened to be the ones he most liked and so we had basically stopped. (I'd had a gin.) You should never tell another woman that your husband has a problematically large penis. She will make a sympathetic face at the time but thereafter she will think about it and think about it and then one day she will go round when you're out and he's in and she will lean on a doorframe and bite her lip.

I couldn't get pregnant and I couldn't stop myself from thinking that it was because his very large penis was causing rearrangements inside me, even though I know bodies don't work like that, or probably they don't. So we tried to adopt this Chinese girl, but it didn't work out. She had a face so simple and perfect that it was like a face sketched in a steamed-up window, but she screamed and screamed when I held her and eventually the lady came back and said The Chemistry Just Wasn't Right.

There is a very large pile of unopened letters on the table by my front door, because I have stopped opening them. It is because opening them often leaves me feeling anxious, whereas not opening them doesn't. Dorothy, gliding by once, noticed the pile. She stopped and fingered it curiously. 'Sweetheart,' she said. 'Some of these have big red capital letters on them, you know.' She beamed. Questioningly. I shrugged. Answeringly. I think that was the day she took away the iron with her. The house is beginning to look as naked and bony as the inside of an umbrella. And I worked hard on it, on its fusses and nice things. We lived well. My mother would say that, when she visited. She would throw her eyes around and say, 'You live well,' in the sort of voice that one might use to say, 'You live like pigs.'

(My husband, you should know, is the kind of man who if someone mentioned pigs in the context of their being dirty would declare smugfacedly that 'pig is in fact a *clean* animal'. He is always pleased to be right.)

You will be wondering why he married me in the first place. I know you will be wondering, because it is the question that is written across every person that we meet together (which is not very many persons). The answer is that my husband stole a very great deal of money from a company that he worked for, and got away with it by having a nervous breakdown. I was a psychiatric nurse at the time, and I looked after him; he married me when he was still quite drugged. What I remember about our wedding is a *great sea of baffled faces* and then at night in bed him blowing outwards like a monster during it – *hoo hoo hoo* – and falling very quickly asleep after. I stroked my own hair in the dark. On the walls there were these sort of plaster horns with pretend flowers coming out of them, and they cast long twisting shadows every time a car went past outside. My mother didn't come to the wedding. She looked at the photos, blew smoke on them, and said, 'You did well,' in the sort of voice that one might use to say, 'You killed somebody.'

I go into the living room and stand staring at the lawn with the leaves trembling on it. It isn't autumn but all the leaves have come off the tree anyway, meaning, I suppose, that it has a disease. While I am through there, I hear some clanking which reveals to me that Dorothy Pugh or somebody to whom she's loaned her keys is taking quite a number of the remaining items out of the kitchen: the microwave, the cafetiere, the egg timer. Under the circumstances I feel that I should look for some help, so I decide to visit the house next door, the one that squats between me and Dorothy. I leave through the front door while the items are being carted out the back. The house next door is occupied by a couple who live as if it is the 1950s. The man has gunky upright hair and the woman is taller than him and big in the hips and wears a lot of lipstick and gingham. She does her hair in victory rolls. She even takes the rubbish out with her hair in victory rolls. The 1950s couple trawl charity shops for period kitchenware as if it's their occupation. I see them returning sometimes, when I'm at the window, and they grin and wave a piece of Bakelite at me. I know from conversations over the years that they do own a DVD player, but grudgingly, and only so that they can glean interior decoration tips from Doris Day films. I don't mind them. Dorothy Pugh wrinkles her nose at them. I suppose they don't have anything she wants.

I knock on the door of the 1950s couple. It takes a long time for the door to be answered and while I'm waiting, I shift from foot to foot and bite the back of my hand. I'm throwing glances over at my house, which is moving about on the inside, like a person who is dreaming. The 1950s man opens the door. His eyes look out at me very wide.

'Hey, mama,' he says to me. There's a smell of heavy smoke behind him.

'Hi. Hi. I live over there. I've —'

'What?'

'Well, I've got a little problem.'

'I know about problems. You should come in,' he says, throwing his arm out behind him. Behind him is dark. I follow him in. We go through the hallway and into their living room. Their house is the same shape as mine, but they still have all of their possessions, which are mostly space-age-looking and pale pink or pale minty green. They have china cats, and plastic flower arrangements, and velvet portraits of heavily-made-up Oriental women. The curtains are all closed even though it's still day outside. His smoke is all over the air. There is something burning in the ashtray. I sit down thumpishly in a space-age-looking pale minty green chair.

'They are taking my things,' I say.

He picks up the thing he's smoking, and sits down too, in a space-age-looking pale pink chair, which squeaks under him. Once he is sitting in it, he sort of waddles it closer to me. Making a lemon-face, he sucks down smoke.

'There's a lot of that goin' on,' he says. 'A lot of disrespect. A lot of HEXPLOITATION.'

'Hex…?'

'Hexploitation's what I call it, mama. There's a hex on the people. They watch us, don't they? They want what we've got. Can't you feel it?'

I'm looking around the room while the 1950s man is talking, and I realise that this is a room in which a woman has not been for some time. The china cats wear lacy caps of dust that make them look like tiny nuns, and there are butts stubbed out in the pots of the fake plastic cacti. There's an old yellowness on everything, and a smell — the kind of smell that happens in a very unclean fridge. He is still talking. 'They won't stop,' he's saying, 'until we're stripped bare.' I flinch at this and turn back to look at him. 'Until we're nude!' he says. He says it like the start of 'noodle'. Laughing with his mouth wide open, he passes the big loose joint to me. I take it awkwardly. His hands free, he claps them both on to my knees, and says it again: 'Until we're *nnnnuuude.*' He is behaving inexplicably, but at the same time there's something distantly familiar about the way he's looking at me. I only place it when his hands begin to travel up my thighs. You would think, wouldn't you, that one of the few advantages of being a woman of no charms whatsoever would be a general immunity from this sort of approach? You'd think a woman like me would be able to be alone with a man, and be safe. It isn't so. Ask any ugly, unkempt woman. Certain men have done a course in us and learned certain things. That we crave attention. That we have no self-protective strategies. That we don't have sharp nails, or jealous boyfriends, and that to the touch with eyes closed, we're not all that different from the good-looking ones who'll give them the runaround and know exactly how to hurt them in the crotch. If you have a daughter, don't bother warning her off low-cut dresses and wiggly walks. Warn her off matted hair and misbuttoned cardigans. Warn her off unplucked brows. They send the wrong message. They say that you're available. They say that you don't care what happens. I draw on the wet end of the joint and the smoke hisses into me and rasps at my palate.

'Where your wife is?' I ask him, mixing my words because of the smoke and also because his hands are rubbing my legs as if he is trying to mould them into a different shape. A fly buzzes near the window.

'Daisy's not my wife,' he says. 'She's a hip lady, a real hip lady, but she's not my wife.' He's pushing his head into my neck as he's talking, and the words are muffled. 'If she was my wife, she'd still be here, wouldn't she?'
I don't have time to ponder this logic, because his hands are trying to get into me and no one has been in that area for a long time and it is making me make noises. His face near my face smells very old, as if he has been underground. The room is getting darker and I'm wondering if there can possibly by now be anything at all left in my house. I struggle him off me. 'This isn't what I came here for,' I say. 'I wanted you to help me.'
    'What makes you think this wouldn't help you?' he says, scrambling at the front of his trousers. While he is plucking out his penis, I whip to my feet, knocking over the space-age-looking pale minty green chair. I run for the door, into the hallway, past the kitchen where the smell is even stronger, to his back door, which is guarded by a plastic hula-hula girl hat stand who swings her grass skirts at me in surprise. I still have the joint in my hand. It's dark over the 1950s couple's scabby back yard. I burst out and land on the pavement outside my house as if I have been spat. There's a big white van there with its motor running. On the side of it it says RIGHT MOVE! in speedy letters with an arrow through them. My husband's car is parked behind it. He and Dorothy Pugh are standing next to it, both smoking cigarettes and smiling.

They have their arms twisted around each other's backs and fronts so that you can't tell whose is whose except that his are hairier. His eyebrows slide up his head and he says, '*There* you are,' as if I am all that was required to complete their happiness.

'It's all done now,' he says. 'It's all as we arranged.'

I nod my head hard, hiding the joint in my fist.

'It looks a bit bare in there!' laughs Dorothy Pugh. 'We're sorry about that!'

'I am quite sure that both of you deeply are,' I say, and we all nod solemnly at each other. Then a deep soreness strikes the back of my throat and tears start to run down my face very fast and in surprising volume. My husband looks distraught. 'It's all as we arranged!' he says again, in protest. Dorothy Pugh's face snaps shut. 'WE NEED TO GO. NOW. DARLING,' she says. In perfect harmony, they both drop their cigarette butts on the gravel and grind them out with their heels. I look up at my husband's big face, and I place the damp crumpled joint in my mouth. 'Will you light this, before you go?' I say.

Looking surprised, he takes out a lighter that belongs to me and lights the end of the joint, while Dorothy Pugh watches with a mouth like an asterisk. And then the van moves off, and they get in the car behind it and go.

Breathing in, I look at my back door, and I look at the 1950s man's back door, which seems to still be trembling. I wonder where Daisy is. The smoke is heavy and soft in my brain. I squidge the roach on the gravel, next to the two dead cigarette butts of my husband and Dorothy Pugh. I go back into my house. They have turned all the lights out before leaving, as if no one lives here anymore, and in the blue dusky living room there is nothing at all but my sewing stool. It's a stool that you can flip open, and inside there are needles. There once was a pouffe and a cushion that went with it, but they have gone. Through the wall, I hear the sound of surf guitars, and then the 1950s man shouting, 'YEAH. That's RIGHT. Fuck YOU, you fucking BITCH.'

The stool looks stupid, all on its own. I sit down on it, to make it feel better. I sit down on top of the needles.

Simon Armitage

The Ice Age

Tuesday the tenth, Wakefield Westgate Station,
seven in the morning, the north end
of the southbound platform,
the platform itself a long promenade
overlooking the prison.

Frost scrimshawed on waiting room windows,
every lungful of air transmuted to silver,
commuters standing about like skittles,
and one skinny kid in jeans and trainers
and a purple glow-stick worn as a choker,
crouched in a patch of useless sunlight,
arms hidden inside his T-shirt,
hugging his body heat, shivering, yawning.
Take off your coat and hold it towards him.

Offer it knowingly, brother to brother.
But he shakes his head, wants nothing from a man
with a train to catch and a coat to spare,
from the hundred-year-old
with the minted smile and retro shoes
and the cuffs and the collar.
He says no, and your blood freezes over.

The Claim

Working the mountain, working the old mine,
operation mind-fuck: I am one man.

All that I am I've sunk into these seams,
everything staked, upholding the old ways,
chasing the grain, dreaming the sleek green dream
of flawless tombstones asleep in the slate.

Some days the ears play tricks on the mind:
bird song, sirens, my own name
launched from the lips of an old flame.

Or some shitty Herdwick ambles along,
a sheep – this far in, this far down – and kneels
on a high ledge over this hollowed dome,
this huge cavern I've christened The Great Hall.

The bedrock sweats. The mountain holds its breath:
not once in its hundred million years
has it filled its lungs or emptied its chest.

I've stopped wearing a watch, just toil and truck
till thinness of blood or thinness of thought
calls time on the shift, then wander back up
to the pinhole of day. This is existence for me,
pinhole days seen through the black pit of the eye.

Stuart Kelly

The Edinburgh World Writers' Conference 2012

Writing to Paul Bowles in the aftermath of the 1962 World Writers' Conference organised by John Calder and Jim Haynes, William Burroughs gleefully exclaimed, 'Looks like we have burned down Edinburgh'. Fifty years later, and under the auspices of the British Council and the Edinburgh International Book Festival, fifty writers from around the world came together in commemoration of the groundbreaking event and to debate again the topics of 1962. Although there was markedly less in the way of literary pyromania, it was still a unique opportunity to survey the state of the art.

The 1962 conference has taken on an almost legendary status. Sexual intercourse, for Philip Larkin, may have begun in 1963 'between the end of the 'Chatterley ban / And the Beatles' first LP', but then he wasn't invited to Edinburgh. Writing in *The Scotsman*, Magnus Magnusson captured the initial fervour: 'Everything went wrong. Crowds were still milling outside the hall long after the advertised starting time. Microphones sulked. The speech of welcome, on tape, didn't materialise. Promised stars failed to turn up. And yet, despite all this – or even because of it – the first international writers' conference to be held at the Edinburgh festival got off to a splendid start'. In an often-quoted letter, Mary McCarthy wrote to Hannah Arendt giving a flavour of the event as a whole: 'People jumping up to confess they were homosexuals; a Registered Heroin Addict leading the young Scottish opposition to the literary tyranny of the Communist Hugh MacDiarmid… An English woman novelist describing her communications with her dead daughter, a Dutch homosexual, former male nurse, now a Catholic convert, seeking someone to baptise him; a bearded Sikh with hair down to his waist declaring on the platform that homosexuals were incapable of love, just as (he said) hermaphrodites were incapable of orgasm (Stephen Spender, in the chair, murmured that he should have thought they could have two). And all this before an audience of over two thousand people per day, mostly, I suppose, Scottish Presbyterians. The most striking fact was the number of lunatics both on the platform and in the public. One young woman novelist was released temporarily from a mental hospital in order to attend the Conference, and she was one of the milder cases. I confess I enjoyed it enormously'.

Angela Bartie and Eleanor Bell have edited and produced an excellent source book and analysis of the Conference, finally allowing critics to assess the impact and ponder the details with a precision hitherto impossible to achieve. It is a tremendous piece of scholarship, and should be on the shelves of anyone who cares about contemporary literature and the avant-garde, Scottish or otherwise. The Conference has been remembered most for the spat between Alexander Trocchi and Hugh MacDiarmid, to which McCarthy refers; in Bartie and Bell's book we can trace the other, perhaps more significant debates which began in 1962. As Burroughs said, the conference 'established the books which had grown out of the underground culture'.

Were one to script the 2012 conference, to begin it with James Kelman pulling out and launching a tirade against the imperialist ambitions of the British Council might seem a tad too easy. Nevertheless it happened. Kelman's philippic was as necessary as the champagne bottle broken on a virgin voyage, and although there were some predictabilities and non-sequiturs in his argument, his essential problem about the 2012 Conference remained noticeably unanswered. Leaving aside Kelman's superannuated gripes about the British Council (though admitting, as he did not, that it used to be called the Empire Marketing Board), the relationship between state acceptance and tolerated radicalism marked the Conference. Over the five days – four in truth, and one watched on-line – I sat in the Royal Bank of Scotland Main Theatre and wondered 'when's this going to actually kick off?'

The 2012 Conference took five topics – 'Should Literature Be Political?', where Elif Shafak introduced Ahdaf Soueif on the first day; then 'Style vs Content', where Ali Smith was introduced by Nathan Englander, (August

18th – coincidentally the day that Alain Robbe-Grillet was born); 'A National Literature', where Irvine Welsh bloviated in front of a wry Ian Rankin; 'Censorship Today', with a graceless Patrick Ness in conversation with the Dutch-Zimbabwean Chika Unigwe; and finally China Miéville chaired by Janne Teller dealing with, at last, 'The Future of the Novel' (on August 21st, and the day that Leon Trotsky was murdered).

Of the speeches, Soueif was inconsequential, Smith impish and stylish, Welsh presumptuous and fakely controversial, Ness hand-wringingly bland and Miéville a sheer delight. Soueif began by stating the obvious – that all literature is political and then moved into a more journalistic mode, describing how events during the Arab Spring meant that, for the time being, there were more important things than writing fictions for Egyptian intellectuals. Smith too began by undermining the proposition (and Englander agreed; separating style and content was like trying to take the eggs out of the cake). Her speech was witty and her conclusions indisputable. Ness took censorship to mean self-censorship: would the authors present, he asked, dare to write about Muhammad? Welsh spoke more about internationalism and global capitalism than nationalism: of which more anon. And Miéville offered some possible futures for the book in the age of open access and 'guerilla editing'. The events themselves were rather peculiar. There was no shouting out, or booing, since the hand-held microphones had to be passed around. When the audience (the readers, the payers) intervened to hear more about what Irvine Welsh thinks (why, I don't know) one of the authors stood up to demand that they, and they alone, had the authority to speak, not the morlocks in the other seats. He may have had a point. He was there as a delegate of an important conference. The audience thought it was actually a Book Festival event.

Where would controversy emerge from? Unlike 1962, there were very few topics one might consider genuinely taboo – when Jackie Kay stood up to declare she was a lesbian there was a round of applause rather than a sharp intake of breath. It seemed there was a stifling liberal, humanist consensus, and only very occasionally did this aspect of the Conference become the subject of the Conference. In the politics debate, for example, Ewan Morrison raised the question of Ayn Rand. *Atlas Shrugged* and *The Fountainhead* were not only political in intent, they had real political consequences – Alan Greenspan and Paul Ryan were both influenced by her philosophy. The Chinese poet Xi Chuan refined the question: how would the debate be different if the question were 'Should Literature Be Fascist?' It was regrettable that there was not more time to explore these questions, especially given the preponderance of Modernist writers (Hamsun, Céline, Marinetti, Pound, Francis Stuart) who had actively espoused far-right views. Literature should be political, it seems, as long as it was 'our' politics.

Given how effectively Ali Smith deconstucted the phoney dichotomy between style and content, it was unsurprising that the debate stalled. That it swerved into much bleating and harrumphing about the success of *Fifty Shades Of Grey* was perhaps less expected, and left a slightly nasty taste in the mouth: the sight of several literary authors bemoaning someone else's success was bad enough; that the profits from the risible 'mommy porn' would become advances for other writers seemed to pass everyone by. The debate nearly became interesting when Alan Bissett suggested that a complex 'style' – by which I assume he meant some combination of modernism, post-modernism, innovation and the avant-garde – might deter some readers. China Miéville swiftly nipped this in the bud, pointing out that second-guessing readers always runs the risk of actually patronising readers (a topic which returned when the discussion moved to Paulo Coelho's attack on *Ulysses*). Miéville maintained that 'rather than giving readers what we think they want, we should be making readers want what we can give', a far more expansive and generous idea of the relationship between reader and writer.

Irvine Welsh hit the headlines for his ill-judged attack on the Man Booker Prize and its supposed bias against Scotland. Curiously, he was citing an article written by Alan Bissett which also stated 'Let's give the prize a further [sic] benefit of the doubt: Scotland, to take one example, has a minuscule 0.2 per cent of the total Commonwealth population, and so, if anything, has been over-represented'. Any survey reliant on population figures is inherently gauche; and ignores, for example, the size of the publishing industry, the availability of routes into publication and presupposes an even distribution of potential 'winners' across the population (with the same figures, one could easily make the claim that the Booker is inherently prejudiced against novels written by postmen, or – I just checked, and this is true – that it helps to have brown eyes). The debate itself was rather more interesting. Once the Scottish question was set to one side (back in 1962, Magnusson had lamented 'this long interior monologue that Scottish writers have been making in public for years and years') some more interesting perspectives arose. Carlos Gamerro raised the question of transnational linguistic homogeneity: Spanish writers have an affinity with Argentinian writers; Brazilian writers with Portuguese writers. It would have been useful to have had the input of two titans of African literature, Ngugi wa Thiong'o and Chinua Achebe, whose disagreement over indigenous languages still has reverberations to this day. Denise Mina very articulately separated out 'situatedness' of narrative with the place of its genesis, another point which could have been more subtly explored.

There was a key moment at the end of the discussion on censorship that threw into sharp relief the differences between where we were perceived to be and where we actually are. When the first Conference took place, it was still illegal to buy a copy of *Lady Chatterley's Lover*, and the Lord Chancellor still had *de facto* censorship in place. Nowadays, as the event on Style and Content showed, the best-selling book in the world is a piece of minor sado-masochistic pornography, freely available in supermarkets as well as book shops. In this context, it is understandable that Patrick Ness would concentrate on self-censorship, concluding his talk by saying 'I don't think the question behind censorship today is any longer should you be able to say these things. Nor is it even a question so much anymore of if you *can*. The question has become, if you *do*.' The Dominican-American novelist and Pulitzer Prize Winner Junot Diaz then revealed from the floor that work by Latino authors was being actively suppressed in Arizona schools. One expected some remarks about Google and China, or even about how the censorship of the market has taken over from the censorship of the State, but this bombshell showed how bizarrely sheltered the authors actually were. There was little time for any debate about how censorship acted as a spur for avant-garde authors in totalitarian regimes to find new ways to express themselves, although a form of 'censorship' was defended by China Miéville (whose contributions increasingly seemed the most incisive and intelligent of the whole affair): citing Enid Blyton's daughter's defence of the removal of the golliwogs from the Noddy books, Miéville went on to reveal that a shop just around the corner still had golliwogs in its window, 'spitting in the face', as he put it, of non-white residents in Edinburgh.

Miéville's speech on the final day referred to Lawrence Durrell's intervention in 1962, where he raised the possibility of a computer generated novel (Durrell claimed a computer in Edinburgh University's linguistics department had already written a poem and would compose its first novel by

Christmas). The figure of the mechanical text has even older precedents: in the preface to Sir Walter Scott's *The Betrothed* he imagined a steam-powered novel-writing loom, and hinted that fake Waverley Novels were already being created by it. Miéville's defence of open access prompted perhaps the most engaged contretemps of the Conference, as Ewan Morrison attacked the utopian 'dot communism' of the enterprise. In this debate, the theoretics of literature were to the forefront. Every text is a remixing of previous texts, as Tom McCarthy argued in his lecture at the Festival last year; all that the digital world does is to lay bare this phenomenon.

It was good that the Conference ended on a note of confusion and perplexity. In the weeks afterwards, I pondered what might have been done differently, and what would inspire a more contentious kind of debate. The decision to revisit the topics of 1962, whilst understandable, rather mired some of the topics in an almost nostalgic tone.

It seems that there are two areas which should be tackled when the Conference returns to Edinburgh in 2013 after touring a number of global literary festivals.

The digital world presents both political and aesthetic challenges. One feasible topic for discussion would be whether the codex book will remain the pre-eminent delivery system for literary texts, and what the actual ramifications of a change to digital means. The 'ownership' of a digital text is still an ambiguous proposition. When Amazon removed copies of Orwell's *1984* from the Kindles of people who had bought it (Amazon had not realised the book was still copyright), it made clear that we don't 'own' a digital text, we have it on a long-term licensed loan. Likewise, the 'kill-switches' in library digital copies, which erase the book after a fixed number of loans, raise pertinent questions of who controls the text. There are major issues to be addressed in terms of falling advances, the desire for free content and how authors ought to be paid for their endeavours. Personally, I rather worry that a group of authors sitting around complaining about their levels of pay might be an unedifying spectacle. Yes, there are concerns about the 'self-cannibalising' nature of the rush for free content, but the issues are more complex and interlocking than the figure at the end of a royalty statement.

Will the digital consumption of texts change the nature of the texts? The question was raised in terms of the Arab Spring, and whether the revolutionary politics had necessitated the creation of new literary forms. The novel came to prominence at roughly the same time as copyright and the idea of personal privacy, and the relationship between novel-reader and novel-writer remains a private interaction. The possibility already exists for texts which break this interaction. Could a digital text be visible, for example, only when more than one person at a time is reading it? The Internet is radically changing the idea of privacy – imagine if your every Google search were made available to your neighbours – and literature needs to respond in some form to these changing ideas. Every technological innovation – whether it is the radio, the cinema film, the television, the video or even the mutoscope – created new aesthetic forms which were dependent on the new technology. It is a moot point whether the digital world has followed the same pattern. Is there an Internet literary art-form? Or is merely an aggregator of former forms, a meta-medium?

It was conspicuous throughout the Conference that the lion's share of the discussion concerned the novel. It would be interesting to see how more representation from poets, from dramatists and from non-fiction writers might change the nature of the debates. In terms of both aesthetic innovation and the vexed question of livelihoods, poetry has very different problems to the novel. Drama, by being inherently collaborative, might have insights into how a less individualistic novel-form might be achieved.

The biggest aesthetic question went unasked. What is post-post-modernism? It may be that writers are actually less interested in these questions than critics, but it seems evident to me that there are a number of strategies being developed that move writing on from the impasse of the kind of postmodernism as practised by Alasdair Gray, Paul Auster and Samuel Beckett. In America, we can see a form of literature uniting genre and literary theory in the works of writers like Diaz, Chabon, Millet, Lethem and Marcus. Writers such as Ewan Morrison and Jenni Fagan have written works which question the novel's reliance on either the individual or the nuclear family. D.T. Max's recent biography of the late David Foster Wallace shows how keenly he struggled with creating a literary form which did not merely describe the problems of an information- and entertainment-saturated reality but sought some cure to it. The relationship between fiction and non-fiction has become increasingly fraught and frayed, in, for example Michel Houellebecq's latest novel or the memoirs of Günter Grass.

Perhaps my highest wish for the Conference is to see whether it can duplicate what William Burroughs saw in 1962: the mainstreaming of literature developing out of countercultural forms. It may be that Situationist recuperation has de-fanged the counterculture, turning it into another marketing and marketable category. But a Conference such as this should be actively seeking those voices. When the Conference comes back next year, I hope there are names I do not recognise.

Jacob Polley

Midnight Show

Afterwards, the fading score
and final print too small to read,
the dark like sleep, and glow that leads
back down the low-lit corridor
and staircase hung with early stars,
to popcorn kettles cooling off,
the cashed-up, blacked-out ticket booth
and frosted doors you drift towards
behind two lovers, slow to leave,
who hand in hand go unaware
across the lobby, through stale air
a childhood's sweetness haunts, achieve
the night at last and briefly turn
to let you pass, a man alone
whose face, like theirs, is not his own
but flickers still with something burned
into his eyes by that long dream
of light that played upon the screen.

Hide and Seek

I wasn't in the chicken coop,
watching. I didn't put my head
through the frayed and dusty loop
slung from the rafter in the pig shed.
I wasn't in the warm, brown egg.
I wasn't in the barrel of rain
or in Grandma Dolly's beige plastic leg.
I wasn't in the rookery. I wasn't in the lanes
that powdered the cow-parsleyed hedgerows
those year-long late summer afternoons.
I wasn't planted. I didn't grow
or constellate. I wasn't field-mushrooms,
milk or mould. I wasn't in the rabbit hole
or under the cowpat. I didn't hang
from the fence with six brother moles.
I didn't do what scarecrows can.
I didn't bark or howl or hoot.
That wasn't me in the frogspawn.
I wasn't brought in on my father's boot.
I wouldn't move like that through a field of corn.
I wasn't under my parents' bed,
listening. I wasn't in the earth
with the bones and broken crockery.
I wasn't in the cold, brown Firth
with the flounders. I wasn't Lockerbie,
Annan or Langholm. I wasn't the South
or the North. I didn't wet the bed.
I wasn't in the snapdragon's mouth

or under the heap of severed heads
or under the heap of turnip heads.
I didn't rust. I wasn't waterproof
or catching. I didn't spread.
I wasn't sunburn or the truth.
I wasn't in the slurry pit.
I wasn't the accordion of baled hay
that drew breath when the string was cut.
I wasn't what I didn't say.
I wasn't the echo of the trout
ringing silently through the slow-
flowing bronze. I didn't shout
and stamp. I wasn't under the snow
that kept me from school. I wasn't slammed.
I didn't leak or scratch or smell.
I didn't go to pieces in a stranger's hands.
That wasn't my voice coming from down the well.

Poem

Invisible
as air
until
a breath
lifts
and makes
palpable
the slyness
of this
snare's
devising.
Strung
in neither
window-
frame nor
ceiling
corner
but here
across
the mouth
this
silver will
hold as
long as the
weaver of
such brief
lucidities
lurks
beneath
the tongue.

Virus

Of course, we all had heinous emissions
for weeks, and for a few days even glory
was emitted heinously by the gold
in galleries where the heinous plunder
we coveted hung, or by small letters
in big books we felt too heinously
short-lived to waste our eyes upon. And then
it was summer and we got brassy
and careless, passing vulpine between us:
his vulpine scent, her tongue sliding vulpinely
over her lips; vulpine, the rooting in bins
by the heinous poor in their zip-up fox pelts,
the vulpine-red tips of the cigarettes they'd re-rolled
from the half-smoked and stubbed-out butts of our own
glowing in the vulpecular late evening gloom.

Caressed awake at weekends, we kept catching
from each other or the TV monstrous
new verbals. Someone caressed shut the front door
so hard the plunder on the wall dropped a right-angle
like a flirt. The lights came on earlier. Overseas
there was high-yield caressing to be done. Then one of us
caressed the road headfirst over the handlebars
of a racing bike and was a long time being retouched
in an antiseptic caressing house. Heinous
struck again for the way an unscarred face
could come back so different; but soon it was
gerbil for tea-towel or horsemeat for colander

after we'd all contracted the same damage
to the temporal lobe, which has lasted
until this autumn of heinous emissions: downpours
and uprisings. Heinous, what's happening in the world
and how softly we're caressed by it, but we've begun
to see more of the moon, its vulpine bib-
flash in the city dark, where we sport hats
with pointy ears and gloves with claws. Out here
we breathe easier now we can see what we say
in smoke, and all feel less gerbil.

Sally Hinchcliffe

Abigail's Father

When Abigail was born her father took her up and looked at her and wondered where she'd come from. Not that he didn't know, of course, he wasn't stupid. It was just that she gave him a look so strange and distant she seemed to have arrived from somewhere else, somewhere unimaginably far away. He stood at the window and watched the sun just touching the rooftops as it rose. Behind him, doctors were rushing his wife away and a nurse would be coming soon to take the baby to be washed and pricked and measured and weighed. For that moment, though, it was just the two of them: her head supported in the cup of his hand, a scrap with milky grey eyes looking inwards at something he couldn't guess at.

Not knowing what else to say, he held her up and turned her so she faced the dawn.

'It's morning, Abigail,' he said. 'You took your time about it.'

He wasn't talking about the delivery so much, although that had been a long and a hard one. His first two girls had been quick. The eldest he hadn't even been there for, the wife's sister had. He'd been away for the weekend, big job up in Manchester, and the baby had been early, caught him on the hop. By the time he came skidding into the ward the baby was washed and dressed and fluffed up, and his wife all smiles. The second one he had attended – sort of – keeping his eyes on the dials and the numbers because they were something he could deal with. But Abigail had tried to come into the world backwards and upside down, had exhausted his wife and him, had worn out two shifts of midwives before she'd arrived. That's why they'd left him there – holding the baby – while they tried to sort his wife out from the blood loss. That's why he found himself alone with her, this strange creature, his girl, his Abigail.

He didn't even know where the name had come from. It was a name from an alphabet book, or a fairy tale, old fashioned – but then, that seemed to suit her. 'An old soul', his Gran used to say, and all at once he knew what she meant. Abigail. As though that had been the name she had always had, the name she was born with.

'All babies look like that,' his wife said, when she was recovered. 'Old like that when they're first born. It wears off.' He didn't remember, but then it had been a while. Abigail had taken her time in more ways than one. His wife had lost two – miscarriages, one after the other, not to be spoken of. Then nothing. Then the endless nine months of waiting for this one, the one he'd secretly tried not to hope would be a boy.

'That's it, though,' his wife said as she lay pale against the pillows. 'No more babies.' No more trying for a boy, she meant. And he agreed because she looked so flat and drained and exhausted and because he had a feeling that the child he was holding in the crook of his elbow might well be enough for them.

He'd thought Abigail might shorten her name – Abby or Gail – or choose one of the other names they'd christened her with, a middle and a spare, to make her passage through school easier. But she didn't, just as she didn't stuff the pale blue specs that the optician had given her into her pocket the minute she walked through the school gates. Abigail was Abigail, and he saw the way she looked at the other children through those pale blue frames with her cool grey eyes, passing judgment. No change there from the looks she gave her dad then. He suspected she did much the same with her teachers because they all seemed a bit nervous with Abigail. When they went to parents' night they said she was a model pupil, but they didn't smile the way they used to with their first two. 'Very bright,' they always said, but he knew that already. She had taught herself to read and the things she asked – well, how do you answer when you don't even understand the question?

'Why can't you ask why the sky is blue like normal kids?' he said once, driven demented by her probing.

'Why is it?' she asked, but he didn't know that either and he shook his head and she shook hers and retreated back into silence and her book.

What he wanted to ask the teachers was if she was happy, but he didn't know how to put it. After all, what kind of parent doesn't know that about their own child?

Abigail's father found himself dreading the day that Abigail would start secondary school. With the age gap, her older sisters weren't going to be that much protection. He had been given hell himself at school for needing glasses and for being too clever for a lad whose own father was a bricklayer. He had taken up smoking and drinking and mucking about to compensate and had successfully failed his exams. He'd ditched the glasses too, no good on a building site for a start. He could see well enough to get by, squinted through the driving test, learned to wing his way through life guessing at what was going on. He followed his dad into the trade but found being a brickie tedious. He'd looked around at where the money was and went for plumbing instead. No messing about with those exams, he got all his qualifications first off and nobody gave you hell at night school.

He worked for himself now, earned enough to be able to send Abigail – well, all his girls – to a private school. It would have been a waste of money with the oldest two, if he was honest with himself. But not Abigail, and it was Abigail he feared for. Abigail with her now wire-wool hair and her wire-rimmed specs and the same challenging gaze she'd been born with. That was going to get her into trouble, surely. Kids were cruel everywhere, though. Even the smart kids in their smart blazers from the private schools; they might not flush your head down the toilet but they knew how to wound with words, and what would they do with a plumber's daughter, however much he earned? So when the time came Abigail stumped off to the local comp as her sisters had before her and he spent the first day trapped in the front room, pretending he was doing his paperwork, watching out the window for her return. He didn't know what he was expecting – torn clothes, tears – but as soon as she rounded the corner into their street he knew he'd wasted a day's work worrying for nothing. She was the same blank tidy self she had been when she left in the morning. If she was ever bullied, or even teased, she never let him know. When once he plucked up the courage to ask her, she just looked at him.

'They're idiots,' she said.

Was that an answer? He didn't know, and he didn't ask again. She had a way of making it difficult to raise an issue, not one she didn't want to talk about.

On Saturdays, Abigail seemed to like to climb into her father's van and accompany him on visits to prospective jobs, or at least that's what she did without complaining whenever he suggested it. At fourteen she was neither pretty nor sweet, and the glasses made her eyes as tiny as frozen peas. Compliments on his daughter died in the throats of his clients as she watched them struggle to finish what they'd started to say. Mostly she sat in his van and read books and waited for him to come out. Her marks were now merely average, her school reports strangely guarded – 'Abigail is not a disruptive influence in class and listens well' – but when he picked up one of the books she'd left in the van he found himself stumbling through the long sentences, feeling his lips moving as he picked through the unfamiliar words.

'Are you doing this at school?'

'Henry James? No, give me a break,' she said. 'At school we're doing *The Great Gatsby*.'

'And what's that like?'

'I read it when I was twelve,' she said, burying herself back in the thick of the book. 'It was pants.'

Abigail grew and grew – not outwards, the way her mother and sisters had, but upwards. She had long feet and more than enough bone – legs and knees and elbows – to make up two of some of the other girls her age. The only thing she ever joined at school was the drama club. She would mention a show in passing, a night or two before it was due to be put on, as though she wasn't expecting them to turn up. He always sat in the front row, his programme pleated in his hand, willing her on. The first two she had minor parts and even he could see that she was out of place – too tall, too loud and then not loud enough, ill at ease. His breath caught in his throat as he watched her. The third one, she didn't appear at all, not till right at the end, at the curtain call when he unfolded his clutched programme to see that it was she who had written the play. She marched onto the stage while the audience pattered hesitantly into applause, as though they were unsure if, after all, they understood what they had just watched. But he didn't care about them. He was standing up, the only one, pounding his hands together with pride and relief as Abigail seemed to look out at him across the lights and smile.

At seventeen she won a competition and her play was performed – just for one day, in the afternoon, before an invited audience – at the National Theatre. Afterwards they stood, plumber and plumber's daughter, playwright and playwright's father, she almost a head taller than him, waiting for people to talk to them. His wife had stayed at home, pleading exhaustion; their eldest had just had a baby, their first grandson. 'And besides,' she said, 'I wouldn't know what to say to all those clever people.' Like he would. Abigail was kissed and darlinged and patronised by everyone in the room and she looked at them all through new, square-rimmed glasses that bent back her hair in two notches above her ears. He noticed the way some of the gush in the room faltered when she fixed her attention on it, conversations trailing off because she had turned her head towards them. When his mobile rang and it was an emergency, a burst pipe, it didn't matter what, he didn't know who was more relieved, him or her.

'I'm a big girl now, Dad,' she said as he made his escape. 'I think I can take a bus home by myself.'

But she didn't come home that night, or the next, or the next. His wife knitted tiny cardigans in white wool and stayed calm. He paced – the hall, the front room, the kitchen – for the whole weekend. She must have waited for his van to leave before she returned because he found her sitting calm and unruffled in the kitchen, drinking tea in her school uniform. She wouldn't say where she'd been. And when her pregnancy began to show, she wouldn't say who she'd been with either. Finally, sighing, she threw the words down like a challenge.

'It was an actor in that play.'

'Are you still seeing him?' But she only made a face that combined contempt with disgust and laughed. He was surprised to feel relieved. She told him nothing more and sailed around the house for the next few months with her bump before her, serene and silent and smiling.

Two months before the baby was due, she disappeared again, this time slipping out in the night with a packed bag and leaving no note. His wife buried herself in the baby they had, the grandson before them, but he could take no delight in it even as he hefted its solid warm weight onto his knee. He was thinking of another baby, born who knows where, living in who knows what squalor, perhaps some actor's bedsit. He had phoned every maternity unit in London but came up against a wall of patient confidentiality. As the day came and went, Abigail's due date, he opened the door each morning with a little burst of hope that he would find the baby on his doorstep, a pair of cool grey eyes looking out from a bundle of pink blanket. It never happened.

Not knowing where else to look, Abigail's father started going to plays. He found a whole world out there of pub theatres and church halls, semi-staged readings and studio workshops. He sipped bad wine at first nights, mindful of his plumber's van standing out like a joke in the car park. He saw the same faces and he was recognised and passed around from group to group like a trophy. The plumber. Man of the people, now there was a joke. His opinion was sought out but even as he muttered something about the rubbish he'd just seen his mind and eyes were always over the shoulder of the person he was talking to, looking out for the tall head that would rise above the gathering like a flower on a stalk. He trailed from clue to clue, seeking out the actors who were in that first play, looking for someone who might return his gaze guiltily, who might have had the coolness and the courage and strength to take on his girl. He saw nobody who fit the bill.

He started reading Abigail's old books, starting with *The Great Gatsby*, working his way back up to the extended sentences of Henry James. He lay on her narrow bed, high up in the attic of the house, his new glasses slipping down his nose, the world around him blurred except for two narrow windows of clarity in front of him. His wife wanted to clear the room, make space for the grandchildren to come and stay. Three of them now, all boys, racketing around the house in the afternoons while his two oldest and his wife sat and gossiped. Their conversation, when he listened, seemed odd to him now – just skating over the surface of things: the weather and celebrities, and endless complaints about their husbands.

'You should leave him,' he said once to one of them in reply, not thinking really, just letting the conversational wheels turn.

'Dad!'

They didn't seem to want answers, not from him, so he went back to just nodding and saying nothing, letting his eyes drift back to the pages of his book. As soon as he decently could he would return to the attic room. Once his wife came and stood silent in the doorway until he looked up and saw her.

'You won't find her,' she said. 'Not if she doesn't want to be found.'

'I know,' he said, but he didn't stop looking. How could he not look for her, his daughter, his Abigail?

He had almost given up, though, the day he overheard someone talking about a radio play. He was tired, that was the thing, too old for it now, too old for everything. Even the business had been handed over to his sons-in-law. He'd sat through an hour and a half of something loosely translated from the Czech, not a laugh in it, not an original thought. They were all filing out when a voice, an actor's voice, said something behind his head about doing a piece for Radio Three. The radio. He'd never even thought about the radio.

'Tricky stuff,' the man said. 'Clever, you know? Cold but clever. Listen out for it, it's called *The Wright*. W R I G H T.'

He turned his head but whoever had spoken was lost in the crowd. *The Wright*. That first programme, that school play, he'd complained to Abigail they'd made a misprint.

'Look,' he said. 'Call this a school, they can't even spell properly. Play wright.'

'That's how it is, Dad,' she'd said. 'Wright. Like wheelwright, shipwright. Someone who builds something. A craftsman.'

'Like me, then?' He'd been joking, but she didn't smile, and for once she hadn't given him that look.

'In a way.'

Two days later he stood in the kitchen, fiddling with his wife's radio, the only one he could find in the house. It wasn't her name in the listing, but then he wasn't expecting it to be. The radio was welded to Capital Gold, never tuned to anything else. He was late, impatient, anxious not to miss the broadcast. His fingers slipped as he inched through bursts of rap and static and inane chatter until the same voice he'd overheard before burst clear and overwhelmed him with the words. Abigail's words, surely Abigail's. Cool and clear, aimed well above the heads of the audience. How could it be anyone else?

He felt something in his chest that he thought was love or pride or anger and he sat down, suddenly short of breath. But it was none of those things, emotions, bursting his heart. It was his heart itself, seizing. Pain crushed his arm and his shoulder and he sat there, not breathing, not realising, just listening to the cool flow of words. He barely cried out as he fell.

His wife stood in the kitchen doorway, her mouth open, turned back into the slender girl that he had married. Her hand went out to the radio, to stem the flow of words but he held her with his eyes and she froze. In his mind he was smiling at her, taking her hand, telling her he'd found their daughter. He gathered her up in his arms and spun her round the room even as the darkness descended and only the words remained. Abigail's words, Abigail's voice, the teenager, the child, her first wailing breath, the strange distant glance of the newborn baby, taking him back with her, back to wherever it was she was from.

Conor O'Callaghan

The Server Room

Even now there are floors where a blue skies
thinktank is thanking its lucky stats,
calendarising all foreseeable windows,
disassembling beneath into Easter's
veritable orangery of hols.

Late evening – a relatively complex
complex of plate glass, workstations idle
but for process in situ, mail arriving –
oversees elements of good practice.
One has no charge to answer. The report said.

An auction site that shall remain nameless
-ly logged into pops one final alert.
Its watchlist's portable Olivetti
(vintage, aquamarine, some signs of use)
is ticking down in red, has been outbid.

There they blow, on the sandstone esplanade,
the gods, the designated parking bays,
barn conversions in the Peaks, wishing well,
whose minuted peaches soon as tabled
spray through local cable in bullet form.

Let the auction fallow. Folly it was,
a romance of keys that goosepimple pages,
of carriages returning with a chink
of light relief and with no memory
to speak of. Leave it grey out. Click Refresh.

Loaves and fishes in the beverage dock
surplus to the shindig for a dray horse
drifting out to grass; swipe-card/lanyard lost;
Morris dancers monthly in the atrium
embedding a culture of celebration

of natural wastage, adapting to scale;
drop-in sessions at the multi-faith centre;
calls for papers 'Theorising Normalcy
& the Mundane'; donations to a present
tense that's leaving for the private sector,

and ripe in bold like fruit unpicked in briar
a sent-from-BlackBerry 'wish you were there'
where *there*'s a chichi Hoxton tapas dive
or that low-tide sandbar from Whitstable
through the Channel they euphemise The Street…

Such gorgeous nubless hubris! Source of which,
a door unmarked this side of History,
becomes a bonnet bee, a bugaboo
at hours like these with all one's colleagues split
and thirsts for loveknots slaked and spirits drab,

and below in sun the tram to Halfway
through the current plan, the ring road
chockablock with external stakeholders,
dominant drivers, opinion formers,
appropriate partners and other 'friends'.

Refresh. And lo! it lands, good news, on cue:
the gospel according to the apostles
of policy, their interim review
via ribbons of white Vatican smoke
or bargeloads towed on virtual canal,

words like the shadows of dirigibles
inching over the closest horizon,
lambs' wolves, bright wolds and dales of old flannel
refurbished for uncertain ages,
great folds of hosannas, angelic notes

all sung suds and bubbles as in some
luxury shower foam infomercial
their mission and vision of pastoral,
maintenance/enhancement of the estate,
emergent patterns, developing fields,

provision for 'real life' experience,
husbandry in selected areas,
arias of a solitary central host
delivered to us from *in excelsis*,
a class of listserv lesser doxology,

our offer's lingua franca reaped and baled
in the graces, airs, of summer's grammar,
green shoots, brand evolution, new markets,
the ale froth of quality, management,
such sumptuous fluff, acres of the stuff,

heavenly bouffant meringues of language,
focus and progression, hope's woolly vowels
working closely with the opalescence
of systems, the knowledge economy,
its argot's luminous opacity

like upholstered immaculate plumage
blooming off brewed hops out towards Burbage,
the remote mother-of-pearl cumulus
of such institutional verbiage
one still finds something oddly moving in.

Refresh. There's nothing left to send/receive.
The cooler is swamped by a ring of empties,
the gridlock seconded to a stream in spate.
The time is now, its last abiding brief
to click upon the happening night without.

Refresh. Now's as pure as any chance
to retrace contraflow the current ocean-bound.
Ascend in clear segments of fluorescence,
past clusters of furniture for chilled confabs,
partitioned space's bureaucratic murk.

Be sure to check there's no one else around.
Then make that door unmarked an echo chamber
to drown the churning of a copy job
resumed from lord knows when, a tripping bus,
the draught's conditional honour of bliss

and listen hard. This interior's hiss
of dehumidifiers, fans and ohms
coursing through each missive's chosen font,
of tangled vines of ampersands, of fronds
of ethernet mycelium/ports,

it rises at that murmurous force ahead,
the rumour blessèd precious few have heard
and fewer glimpsed, a falls at altitude
that pilgrims – handfuls, barefoot, far between,
in search of altered states – give credence to.

This is the server and the server's place
of worship's working templates. Praise the here
where mountains float above a pea-soup mist
and all that blue skies thinking has been saved.
Pray to the deities of eternal code. Refresh.

Up here on the lam, the limb of oneself,
form a cup of digits/palms and wait
for data like rain meltwater cold
to pool to brimming point, to cascade down.
Drink. Be whole again beyond communication.

Frances Leviston

Spectacle and Speculation
Reflecting on *Elizabeth Bishop in the Twenty-First Century: Reading the New Editions*

When Elizabeth Bishop died in 1979 at the age of 68, she had published four books containing seventy-seven poems between them (seventy-four if you count 'Four Poems' as a single piece). Her last, *Geography III* (1976), had just nine poems in it, among them two of her best ('Crusoe in England' and 'The Moose') and the villanelle 'One Art', certainly her most well-known. The *Complete Poems* (1983) added another seventeen published but uncollected works, as well as juvenilia and translation. So it is that Bishop's considerable reputation, encompassing both scholarly and popular renown, has until recently rested on fewer than a hundred original poems.

After the early work done by Anne Stevenson and David Kalstone, a second wave of critical interest was triggered by Vassar College's acquisition of Bishop's papers in 1981, and by the publication of her *Complete Poems* and *Selected Prose* in 1983 and 1984 respectively. Dozens of books and articles appeared in the 1990s, and the crowd-sourced critical bibliography on the centenary website lists a daunting 1,795 items, though admittedly some of these make only passing reference to Bishop ('Big-Time Football at Harvard, 1905: The Diary of Coach Bill Reid' offers limited illumination). At the centre of what amounts to a third wave of criticism is 2005's *Edgar Allen Poe and the Juke-Box*, a volume of unpublished drafts and fragments edited by Alice Quinn. *Elizabeth Bishop in the Twenty-First Century: Reading the New Editions*,[1] discusses extensively the impact of *Edgar Allen Poe* on Bishop's reputation, and also considers two further volumes of primary material that have appeared since the millennium: *Words in Air*, the complete correspondence between Bishop and Robert Lowell, and *Poems, Prose and Letters* (all Farrar, Straus and Giroux).

Paradoxically, the exponential increase in both critical interest and primary materials is also the central problem with which Bishop studies currently wrestles. Thomas Travisano, one of the editors of *Elizabeth Bishop in the Twenty-First Century,* writes that '[t]he Bishop canon is still expanding, at a rate that often seems to exceed her rate of production while she lived.' Questions remain about whether this expanded canon is actually representative of Bishop, or whether it does, in some fundamental and disconcerting way, 'exceed' her. The title helpfully embodies this anxiety. On the one hand, Bishop remains a formative presence for many poets; on the other, she didn't survive into the twenty-first century, and so it seems to posit an alternate dimension in which her lifespan is unnaturally prolonged. But how present, and how malleable, is Bishop's career to us still, and why should we want to extend it?

The obvious reason is that Bishop studies has a vested interest in expanding Bishop's body of work: the academic mill has grown so large that new grist is needed. The draft poems included in *Edgar Allen Poe* lie at the centre of these debates. Their publication divided critics. While some welcomed wider access to materials that had previously only been available in archives or scholarly papers, others – notably Helen Vendler in the *New Republic* – were concerned that publication of these imperfect drafts diluted Bishop's notoriously high editorial standards (despite their publication being in accordance with Bishop's will, since she gave her executors the power to decide). What had been a carefully controlled canon doubled in size overnight, and much of the newly-available work was markedly inferior: Vendler called the poems of *Edgar Allen Poe* the 'maimed and stunted siblings' of Bishop's published work.

Jonathan Ellis's essay 'Alice in Wonderland: The Authoring and Editing of Elizabeth Bishop's Uncollected Poems', which opens the book, includes a surprising confession: 'Bishop is not always the best judge of her poetry. This is not the easiest thing to write. It is perhaps one of the last taboos among Bishop critics.' This intimate tone of disclosure guides the reader's attention to the point at which critical propriety shades into the proprietorial: those speculating on the Bishop estate, so to speak, are at risk of upsetting one self-appointed guardian or another, but Ellis encourages their activities, stressing the need for 'other ways of reading her work'. Ellis's own exploration of *Edgar Allen Poe* rejects the usual complaints and instead demonstrates the extent of Quinn's critical interventions (for which he argues co-author status ought to be conferred) and the essential instability of Bishop's work and persona: 'I wonder whether Bishop ever considered any poem or poetic statement complete.'

Other contributors are not so nuanced in their search for a novel interpretation. As part of the continuing excavation of what Victoria Harrison called Bishop's 'poetics of intimacy', Angus Cleghorn alerts us to the prevalence of electrical cables and power-lines in Bishop's work, and connects these to the new sexual energy in her Florida poems. This is perceptive, but Cleghorn spoils it by claiming too much, and the essay overbalances into absurdity. Tying himself in knots about technology, nature and time, Cleghorn interprets the 'intelligent green light in the harbor' at the end of the draft poem 'Dear Dr. –' as an 'alien technological prophecy', whatever that might be. A later summary sentence attempts to orientate the reader, with grotesque results: *The Complete Poems* provides intricately innovative poems that point out limited perspectives while expanding ethical imaginations of the future, whereas Quinn's book enables readers to thoroughly explore the dream workings of a poet bursting from the libidinal confines of her time, swinging by green vines through wires of sound and light to transmit electricity for an erotically ample future.' Cleghorn's quest for novelty results in the undignified and unconvincing spectacle of Bishop as a neon erotic dream Tarzan.

Cleghorn does at least contrast the *Complete Poems* with the 'dream workings' of *Edgar Allen Poe*. Other contributors, by using the same critical vocabulary to discuss both volumes, fail to register (or even deliberately occlude) the categorical difference between Bishop's poems and drafts. Charles Berger, Heather Treseler and Lloyd Schwartz are particularly guilty of over-estimating unfinished poems that depend for their significance on the published work. Berger subjects the tentative 'Where are the dolls who loved me so…' to a detailed psychoanalytic reading, arguing that Bishop's dolls, with their 'blank crotches', offer a parodic revision of Freud's 'The Uncanny'. This is potentially interesting, but the poem in question is so slight that it cannot bear the weight of such scrutiny. Treseler's essay on Bishop's epistolary poems makes a stronger case for a psychoanalytic reading, but fails on the same terms as Berger when it treats the fragments 'I see you far away, unhappy' and the aforementioned 'Dear Dr–' as exemplary works. Here is a passage from the latter:

The past are from

memories

all those photographs waters
                    con
manufacture, their fluences
[indecipherable line]

with all the photographs & notes
            manufacturing fluences every minute
            rotogravure
with the photographs water
    manufacturing fluences every minute –

Treseler writes: 'The *in*-fluence of tears, the *con*-fluence of harbor waters, and the black-magic force of false memories are all valences of meaning in Bishop's fragmentary verse.' The give-away phrase is 'fragmentary verse', which suggests that Bishop was deliberately constructing a fragmented aesthetic. Lorrie Goldensohn more accurately diagnoses such reiterative notation as Bishop testing how to cast her lines, a process Goldensohn calls 'this little stutter of the poet's mind at work'. The most troubling of the over-readings is given by Lloyd Schwartz, who explains how he stole 'Breakfast Song' from Bishop's notebook when she was wheeled from her hospital room for an X-ray in 1974. Schwartz makes big claims for 'Breakfast Song', saying it possesses 'poignant Shakespearian resonance'. It is of course manifestly in his interests to cement the poem into the canon and thus place himself as far beyond reproach as Lavinia Dickinson or Max Brod.

By giving such weight to the drafts, *Elizabeth Bishop in the Twenty-First Century* seeks to expand our sense of Bishop into areas mapped by her unfinished work, claiming her as a political poet, an explicitly lesbian poet, or a poet of greater emotional vulnerability than the *Complete Poems* would suggest. But Bishop's unfinished poems do not represent her as a poet; rather, they represent the kind of poet she attempted and failed to become. To take just one of the drafts on which several scholars lean, 'Vague Poem (Vaguely love poem)' does indeed possess an extraordinary sexual frankness, and its explicit identification of geological structures with the female form strengthens our understanding of the intimacy between landscape and love in Bishop's work; but the poem is not achieved, and it stands finally as a testament to her failure to confront lesbianism directly in verse. There is beauty in the poem, particularly in the concluding stanza, but it is a Lawrentian ecstasy of repetition not distinctively hers:

> Just now, when I saw you naked again,
> I thought the same words: rose-rock, rock-rose...
> Rose, trying, working, to show itself.
> Forming, folding over,
> unimaginable connections, unseen, shining edges.
> Rose-rock, unformed, flesh beginning, crystal by crystal,
> clear pink breasts and darker, crystalline nipples,
> rose-rock, rose-quartz, roses, roses, roses,
> exacting roses from the body,
> and the even darker, accurate, rose of sex —

The vacillating syntax is not commensurate with Bishop's brilliantly tenuous sentences elsewhere: here, again, it is a compositional stutter. In 'roses, roses, roses', we see the dimming of intensity hinted at by 'unimaginable connections, unseen'. The poet's vision fails her in this new terrain.

That we need not resort to promoting unfinished works to canonical status in order to find new ways of reading Bishop – not even as a politicised poet – is demonstrated in fascinating essays by Peggy Samuels and Gillian White. Samuels explores the impact of Alexander Calder's sculptures on Bishop's poems. Bishop was particularly interested in Calder's mobiles, constellations of small objects in motion driven by motors or hand-cranks, a couple of which were owned by Bishop's Brazilian partner Lota de Macedo Soares. In convincing readings of 'The Armadillo', 'A Cold Spring' and 'Arrival at Santos', as well as two draft poems, Samuels clearly outlines the affinity Bishop felt for these lively works of art, and how they helped her model the movements in her poems. In 'Arrival at Santos', we see Bishop 'setting disparate levels of certainty and hesitation in the speaker's mind in a field of objects that move with varying degrees of certainty'. Calder's mobiles often had objects meet one another with a 'robust bump' in mid-trajectory, an effect replicated by Bishop when the boat hook swings into view and lifts Miss Breen into the air: 'Like Calder, Bishop links suspense in time (the always being poised in one's own mental motion for the next event that will enter the "scene") with suspense in space (traveling on a trajectory that will "hit" or "be hit").'

Gillian White argues that *Questions of Travel* represents a midcentury critique of American society. With her famous coolness and reticence, Bishop has often been accused of a privileged withdrawal from the political sphere, but White shows these qualities to be a politicised response to the immodesty and vulgarity of 1960s advertising culture. Bishop felt that this vulgarity had found its poetic equivalent in the willingness of poets like Sexton and Snodgrass to commodify their personalities. In her own work, she created an 'interpretive space' that would quietly protest this excess of emotion and self-consciousness. Bishop's 'destabilisation of the grounds of sympathy' casts doubt on the sincerity of any speaking voice. Reading against familiar interpretations of 'First Death in Nova Scotia' as a poem about childhood trauma, White says, 'the fantastic and symbolic images to which the child resorts are less imaginative deflections of the difficulty of her cousin's death, than indices of how children inherit culture, including sentimental discourse.'

That both White and Samuels manage to draw illuminating readings from Bishop's published poems shows how much they still have to offer a resourceful reader. Other critics have to circumvent academic propriety to generate a new interpretation, allowing themselves to speculate on the significance of events that never happened, on books that Bishop never wrote, or on a life she did not lead. Discussing Bishop's correspondence with Flannery O'Connor, George S. Lensing writes: 'Had they met, they would surely and quickly have warmed to the utter unpretentiousness of the other.' There is no way of knowing this. The fact that Lowell and O'Connor got along, for example, is no guarantee that Bishop would have had similar feelings: there were plenty of poets about whose company they disagreed, including Ezra Pound. Lensing's venture is indulgent but harmless; Richard Flynn's speculations are more insidious. Writing about *Words in Air*, he concludes: 'one can't help thinking that, had they lived longer, Bishop and Lowell undoubtedly would have given us more poems concerning "the experience of life", poems that would further articulate heartbreak and loss without giving in to self-pity.' The truism that Bishop and Lowell's future poems would have concerned 'the experience of life' is used to smuggle through the assertion that their writing lives would have culminated in precisely the poems of 'heartbreak and loss' that Flynn's argument requires. The speculative nature of Flynn's proposition makes it impossible to counter with anything except a further speculation: given Bishop's distaste for confessionalism, she may have retreated ever further from it.

Equally problematic is Francesco Rognoni's essay on 'Visits to St. Elizabeth's'. Explaining that the poem was first published in a special issue of an Italian journal dedicated to Pound, and that Bishop later changed 'tragic' to 'wretched', Rognoni writes, 'One may speculate that Bishop decided only in the nick of time [to submit the poem] and, perhaps pressed by [the editor] Rizzardi, sent a version of the poem that was still unsatisfactory.' The alteration of one word is not sufficient evidence to support this disparaging claim. Rognoni then dismisses without explanation another scholar's argument that 'Visits' was already finished by 1951, making his own guess about its composition: 'The self-generating form seems to require that the poem was written in a hurry, almost unthinkingly: almost in the same way in which Bishop must have walked the long and noisy corridor to Pound's St Elizabeth's quarters.' This is silly. Bishop's processes admit of more variety than we commonly believe, but no published poem of hers was ever 'written in a hurry, almost unthinkingly', and formal ease cannot be taken as proof of effortless creation. In any case, Rognoni soon contradicts himself by showing that the poem took several shapes before settling on its published incarnation. Later, he wonders whether Pound and Dorothy read 'Visits', offering more speculation before he finally admits that 'they may well have disliked it, but no reaction is extant.' Quite.

Just as critics of Seamus Heaney often adopt his 'soundings', 'amplifications' and other rhetorical quirks, the origins of the speculative trend in Bishop studies may lie in Bishop's own work, with its characteristically hazardous and contingent tone: for example, 'He appears to be – rather, to have been – a unicyclist-courier, who may have met his end by falling from the height of the escarpment' ('12 O'Clock News'), or 'He's still / asleep. Even awake, he probably / remains in doubt' ('Twelfth Morning; or, What You Will'), or the second half of 'Questions of Travel', which is cast almost entirely in a conditional tense. However, Bishop's playful description of how things 'would have been' is usually a way of showing how they are: the poems' 'speculations' are nothing of the sort. Scholars wondering how Bishop's career might have developed miss this subtler point.

Travisano is the main proponent of the speculative method. His essay of 'speculative bibliography' opens with a daring proposition: 'Imagine, if you will… Elizabeth Bishop, at the age of sixty-eight, visits a brilliant Boston cardiologist and receives timely medical treatment and advice, thereby avoiding what might have been her sudden death…' The essay goes on to posit a hypothetical *Geography IV,* the book Bishop might have published had she lived into the 1980s, which would show 'a new directness, sometimes even a certain rawness or indelicacy, emerging from the Vermeer-like surfaces of a poet [reviewers] no longer refer to as Miss Bishop.' Based on the four new poems Bishop had finished by the time of her death and the drafts with which she was engaged, Travisano delineates five possible thematic areas for the book: Brazil Reconsidered, Childhood Memories Extended, The Further Art of Losing, Abstract Self-Portraits, and Poems of Love and Sexuality. Sympathetic as this taxonomy proves, it is undermined by Travisano's decision to favour a title of his own invention over the working titles Bishop gave in her 1977 Guggenheim application: *Grandmother's Glass Eye* and *Aubade & Elegy*.

The most persuasively speculative essay is the one that concludes the book, in which Christina Pugh considers developments in Emily Dickinson studies as an indicator of where Bishop studies might be heading next. Since the publication of Dickinson's manuscripts in facsimile format, Pugh argues, she has been 'co-opted' by theorists of experimental poetry who seized on the fascicles as 'open texts', ignoring the fact that they were written in traditional metres, and instead fetishising the 'mark' of her variant writings. This serves the same ends as those more radically biographical critics who insist one cannot read Dickinson's letter-poems properly without reference to the dead crickets and dried flowers by which they were accompanied: Dickinson's value is fastened to the materiality of her writing and domestic circumstances. Pugh sees a similar, worrying trend in Bishop studies, whereby the scholarship is becoming archival and manuscript-based rather than literary and interpretive. She is also concerned about critics co-opting Bishop into a postmodern aesthetic (Treseler's 'fragmented verse') that makes little sense in relation to the finished poems. The danger is that Bishop's real achievements will be circumscribed and obscured under the guise of widening her appeal.

The years to come promise many more avenues of access to Bishop; indeed, *Elizabeth Bishop in the Twenty-First Century* has already been outpaced by Joelle Biele's *Elizabeth Bishop and the New Yorker,* which appeared too late to be considered for the book. Travisano is writing a new literary biography; a collection of essays from the Bishop centenary conference in Nova Scotia is due to appear next year; a *Cambridge Companion to Elizabeth Bishop* is on the way; and a film about Bishop's time in Brazil, *The Art of Losing*, starring Miranda Otto as Bishop and Glória Pires as Macedo Soares, is currently shooting on location in Samambaia and Rio de Janeiro. Given such investment in new presentations of Bishop and her poetry, the questions of how and why we read her, and of how her literary afterlife should be managed, will only become more urgent.

Note

1. *Elizabeth Bishop in the Twenty-First Century: Reading the New Editions* Eds. Angus Cleghorn, Bethany Hicok and Thomas Travisano. University of Virginia Press, 2012.

Gary Allen

Dream as Big as Africa

My mother can't walk anymore
she wants to give up
her legs are swollen like an old cow elephant's
with age and heat and dehydration.

When I adjust the tight bandages
the yellow pus runs through my fingers
from the ulcers

she wants to cry out
she wants to let the dry dust blow over her
she wants the sky above her to fill with cold stars:

I awake in a room that is not the room
I was born in
or locked in to be quiet –
my legs are fine for the moment

in the cool evening cackling hyenas
rip and twist and tear
the soft meat from her womb

vultures pick at the eyes and bones
in my dream she asks for water
a heel-print of muddy water

in my dream I am useless
as an unmarried man
as a man without offspring.

My mother's legs each weigh a ton
her eyes are wet
yet we both laugh at my carelessness.

In this room I am beginning to see the dark
in this darkness I hear her walk again
like teaching seven children to walk for the first time
she is bumping into chairs and bookshelves.

The Beautiful Game

Mexico, Mexico, my father cried
as the blinding sun bubbled the paint from the window-sill
and his two thigh-waders flopped over
like drunk dogs on the back step
their sewage stink filling the room

from mending pipes fractured by car-bombs:
and everything was bully-beef before the telly
and every shout was, Shut your face!

as the sun beat down on the stadium waves:
Where is Mexico anyway? up past Templeton's Garage
the other side of the Sandy Row, a lamb chop on a plate

Emiliano Zapata, the Rio Grande, Geronimo
the soldiers crouched in the garden hedges
the policemen listening to radios in concrete sangars

the bruises on my face like big purple poppies
ankle plastered like an Alamo wound
from the gang who had caught me coming up the estate
as I left the only Protestant house on the Sierra Madre

fuck football: years later in Amsterdam
a friend took me to a back room in a seedy hotel
where I saw my first snuff movie

though I wasn't sure if it was real
a Mexican girl butchered on the bed of a filthy room
the bones pushed through the skin
cold and methodical, like my father shouting for England.

Nina

I see your father among the cabbage patches
now that he is old he has become an imbecile
hoeing the ground, wearing a broken straw summer hat

he fears his mind is running away like Canada,
his sister died thinking of Canada

Canada is a large blank map on their bedroom wall
Canada is an airman's uniform at the table –

the fool, he should have stayed among his aerodynamic books,
he thought he knew you
I thought I knew you.

Nina, do you still have the twisted straw fertility dolls
you bought in an Indian village in Oaxaca?
like thin money in a displaced Nigerian's pocket-book
like decadence in an East German's blue eyes
the dead eyes of straw dolls and Indians
and the men who lie broken-minded on your divan.

Persian flower, mouth, mother
John is dying from end-stage multiple sclerosis
you have known him for a long time
and fuck him though he is crying:

they are sending them to die now in square boxes
down in Switzerland with pills and plastic cups and digital television
out beside a busy road and industrial estate
like slaughter houses for swine –

when I was a boy Sunday was a sin of waste
counting the Blue Circle Cement trucks
as they passed the high level-crossing like blurred clouds
and I knew then that the mind was big enough
to contain the randomness of the universe

but nothing is real in Berlin my love
the film companies have moved it to Prague or Krakow
like the emptiness in your suburban Berlin garden
in this middle-aged body these handicapped men
pay for with their pocket-money
in your father's memory-box
as he tries to remember what he is doing there.

I am sick of Berlin, the tired old sex-worker
I want to give everything back to the luggage-locker
the bicycle-clips, petrol bombs, leg callipers,
counting-cards, truss, condoms –
I want to tidy my mind like a morning room with a little sun.

Thomas Legendre

Double Time
An excerpt from *Living in the Past*

If I draw a circle it doesn't matter where I start, so let's begin with Aaron appearing from the future. How does a time traveller arrive? By buzzing the entryphone. It halts me during Bach's Passacaglia in C minor for organ – or rather, a piano transcription that seems too thin, too sterile – and I rise from the bench humming the final variation, trying to give it some life. But I stop short when I hear Aaron's voice bristling with static. This can't be good news. He's supposed to be in Mid Argyll. As his footsteps come up the main stair I think maybe the next phase of his Great Dig was postponed and he lost his keys in a Neolithic ditch. And then the sight of him sends me backing into the sitting room. He recites my favourite colour, my lucky number, my comfort foods, my shoe and dress sizes – as if I need convincing, when in fact the problem isn't that I doubt who he is, but that I immediately believe it. Yes, it's obvious. My future is his past. Although it's April of 1988 for me, it's November of 2006 for him – or almost November. Halloween Night. That's when our son will stay home with me, he says, while he takes take our daughter trick-or-treating despite my disapproval so he can introduce her to his American childhood ritual, his annual allowance of junk food and fright. I can't imagine myself frowning at such a harmless thing, which is partly why it seems like a different woman in that time. An alternate self. The mother of two children. I'm already suspicious of her. Where does she begin? Where do I end? But I'm getting ahead of myself. I'm here. I'm now. If I draw a circle, it doesn't matter where I start.

'But you need to know it's really me,' he says. 'And I can prove it. The first time we met was at that pub near Bristo Square. You were upset about playing the Rach 5 and I told you…' He stops himself, clenching his eyes shut. 'No, no. Wait. Anyone could know that.'

He turns away and grips the mantel, in the throes of some internal debate, then turns back and starts reeling off details about something that happened to me before that – a private trauma I've never shared with anyone. Proof. Evidence. He needs to convince himself that I'm convinced. He needs to believe that I believe.

'Aaron?' I wave him down. 'This isn't necessary.'

'But you locked the door behind him,' he says, carrying on, 'and you sat there hugging your knees until dawn when you could walk home safely and you couldn't even bring yourself to tell Clare or Isobel afterwards, instead making up some story about, what was it, he vomited and passed out. It was your first and last one-night stand. Am I right?'

His face is both familiar and strange. There's a wider spread to his features, the continental drift of age, but otherwise he seems recast with sharper angles and ridges, with deeper definition. The endearing little curve to his lower lip is more pronounced, his hairline reduced to a close-cropped style that actually suits him better. It's the haircut he should have had from the beginning. I hesitate to mention it because I'm afraid he's going to say it was my suggestion. The other Violet. A deep unease comes over me, unreasonably, at the thought of her.

'Violet, please. Am I right about this?'

I manage to nod.

'Have you shared that experience with anyone?'

I manage to shake my head.

'Anyone at all?'

I close my eyes to absorb not the fact but the feeling of it. A new time signature.

'I know it must be strange to have me describe it this way… like watching your own dream on television. But you'll tell me in a few years. At a recital one night you'll see someone who resembles him and you'll confess the whole thing afterwards, right here in this room. Except it's not really a confession because you didn't do anything wrong. I should mention that now, ahead of time, to pre-empt some of the guilt. Because the guy tried to rape you, for Christ's sake, so don't be ashamed of that and I *still* want to track him down and break his kneecaps, which you'll attribute to my crude notion of Appalachian justice. If memory serves.'

And his accent has changed. Those hints of southern comfort, those drawling vowels – all tempered to British speech. The sound of him, the sense. Yes, it's the man he will be in eighteen years. One of my legs is trembling like a bow string and I have to collar it with both hands to make it stop.

He comes forward. 'Are you all right?'

I step back and knock into a lamp. He lunges and catches it before it falls, and then looks at it oddly as he sets it back.

'Tessa broke this. She was crawling under the table and –' He glances at an empty corner of the room. 'The table we're going to buy after we have the flat repainted. In 1996, I think.'

'Good thing you caught it, then.'

His attention snaps back to me, flummoxed by the comment until it takes hold and he laughs. He nods for a moment. Then his eyes widen with mischief. 'Hey, should I smash it and see what happens?'

'Please don't. It's hard enough living in an unfurnished rental – and excuse me, but how are we going to buy this flat if we can barely afford the rent?'

He hesitates, sensing a tripwire. 'Did I say we bought it?'

'You said we repainted it. Seven years from now.'

'Oh. Well. Don't worry about that. It's not the sort of detail that matters.'

I fold my arms. 'As opposed to what, my shoe size? Which you got wrong, by the way.'

'Your shoe…' He taps a finger against his temple. 'Ah, right. Before the children you're a five, not a five-and-a-half.'

'Pardon?'

'Because your feet swelled with the pregnancies.'

'You mean, permanently?'

He shrugs.

'Leave off, Aaron. Time travel is more plausible than *that*.'

He seems to drop a notch. It's all crucial to him. Endings and beginnings, cause and effect. With renewed desperation he starts patting himself down, as if searching for a futuristic calling card. But what can he offer? He isn't wearing any silver lamé. No spacey designs or insignias. Just a jumper with a hole in the shoulder, a collared shirt, jeans. The trainers are a type I've never seen before, but that doesn't mean much. He could be from any time, any place. He doesn't even have a wallet. The only artefact he can produce is an electronic domino, which apparently is a phone.

'Will you stop that, please?'

'I'm trying to provide hard evidence.'

'Hard evidence of what? That mobiles are shoddy in 2006?'

He holds it up. 'The supporting technology doesn't exist yet. If you brought a radio back to the eighteenth century and switched it on, it wouldn't –'

'But it *doesn't* switch on.'

'Or maybe the circuits were fried in the…' he gestures vaguely and rubs his forehead, 'I don't know, the time warp or whatever you want to call it, because it sure as hell did something to my nerves. In fact, I thought that was the problem at first. It felt like a concussion. A seizure, maybe. Except the weather was different. The daylight. The trees budding. I realised it was spring. I could taste it in the air. And then right outside our building I saw…' He trails off, his eyes magnetised by something across the room.

I swivel and follow his gaze, but don't find anything worthy of fascination. The stereo and records, the old armchair, the telephone on a pedestal that my uncle gave me when his art gallery shut down for good. I turn back to him. 'You saw what?' I ask.

He walks over and puts his hand on the phone as if he doesn't quite believe it exists. 'That would be the real test,' he says.

'Pardon?'

'No room for doubt after that.'

'What are you talking about?'

He picks up the receiver, but then immediately slams it down again and steps back with his hands bridged over his mouth, his face losing resolution.

'Hey,' I say, coming up to him. 'It's all right. I'm here.'

He seems to fold at my touch, collapsing with the emotional weight of it. He takes hold of my hand and lifts it to his face. I trace the etchings around his eyes. The extra weather in his skin. As I settle against him I realise he has lost bulk all over, his body condensed and economised. There's a firmness to his chest, a harder texture to his arms. Does he exercise now? I try to imagine him at the gym, substituting fitness for youth – a youth still intact in the other Aaron, working on an excavation three hours away from here. I run my hands all over him, him but not-him, finding the differences, the octaves between one and the other like playing the Passacaglia in a lower register to bring out the resonance the way it always does with Bach except I can't find it, whatever it is, missing from the transcription because the notes are as right as his fingers pressed to my shoulders but it still doesn't sound true. Do I still think this way in the future? Am I always this strange? But when I pull back to ask him, I find the full presence I've always anticipated without realising it, his face in mine.

'Ultra-Violet,' he says. 'It's you.'

There's no reason to stop what happens next. He's here and there, now and then. By the time I work his shirt off I've discovered a new scar on his shoulder, don't try to guess how old, and a mild subsidence in his body. But it doesn't matter. Oh, it really doesn't matter. He hits notes of pleasure in me that I didn't even know were there, new pitches on my scale. Of course he has an unfair advantage. An extra eighteen years of practice. But the thought disappears as he carries me across the threshold of our bedroom like it's our wedding night. Do we get married? I grip his hand against the mattress at one point and feel a wedding ring. Well, then. I'd better say yes when he proposes. It's like our honeymoon with all this messy raunchy tenderness.

After we pull apart I stretch out in a highness and sizzling purity, all nerve endings and open strings. The window displaying a slideshow of sunlight through clouds, the howling raw motions of sky. A breeze sighing through the dormant fireplace. Traffic rumbling faintly like a waterfall in the distance. Everything acute and true. His leg still draped over mine. An octave occurs when one pitch has exactly double the frequency of the other. But this is another harmonic. A different sequence of semitones. A perfect fifth. Yes. The interval above the root of all major and minor chords and now excuse me while I smile.

He slides out of bed and starts gathering up his clothes. 'This isn't a coincidence.'

I turn toward him. 'What?'

'The date.'

'You mean, Good April Fool's Friday?'

He gives me a perplexed look.

'That's the joke you made when you called last night. Or maybe I should say eighteen years ago? Because it's Good Friday and April Fool's Day, together at once – which proved, you said, that the Resurrection was really just a prank that got out of hand. Why else would they celebrate the occasion when the saviour was whipped and beaten and nailed to a cross? If that's a good Friday I'd hate to see a bad one.'

He holds still for another instant, blinking the thought away. 'I'm talking about spring 1988. Kilmartin Glen. The excavation at Inbhir. Right now I'm discovering that it's not only a chambered cairn, but also…' He breaks off. 'I'll tell you – I mean, *he'll* tell you all about it when he comes home tonight.'

'Lovely. Something to look forward to. But why is that a coincidence?'

'I go back there in 2006.'

'And?'

He shakes his head. A forbidden topic. After stepping into his jeans, though, he gives me a thoughtful look. 'This weekend he's going to mention a woman named Siobhan. Pottery expert. He fancies her. Over the next few weeks he's going to discover that the feeling is mutual and he'll be tempted. He won't admit it, of course, but it will be obvious. And here's the important thing: It won't go beyond flirting and innuendo. Nothing is going to happen. So relax about it, ok?'

'Ok,' I say, lying on my side, trying to seem nonchalant. 'Anything else?'

But then he halts and reaches for something on his bureau – the mug he won at a state fair when he was a boy. Another casualty of the years between us, no doubt. Is he going to blame our daughter for this one as well? As I watch him run his fingers over the raised lettering I can't help recalling that moment at the telephone. Who was he going to call? Before I can ask, though, he sets the mug back and, still naked from the waist up, strides out of the room. I lean over and watch him through the doorway of his study, examining all the drawings and photos tacked to the wall – the collage he hopes will provoke some kind of insight. And the Ordnance Survey map that he marks with the locations of all known rock carvings in Kilmartin Glen like a general plotting troop movements. I am under solemn oath under penalty of death not to tell his co-workers for fear he will be mocked mercilessly. Because he is convinced the rock carvings occur not at random locations but at natural thresholds of the landscape, with the motifs taking on greater complexity at key approaches. Furthermore, he says, they have a systematic relationship to the cairns and standing stones along the floor of the glen. They lead you to those sites. They guide you in. They bring you down.

They brought me down into boredom, long before Aaron's time, when I first saw them on the way to a family holiday in the Hebrides. The diversion was Dad's idea – some pagan viscera to offset the tepid encounter with St Columba that he knew Mum would insist upon once we reached Iona. At least that's how I understand it now. And what was the great heritage of Kilmartin Glen? A few standing stones. Some rock piles resembling igloos where prehistoric corpses had supposedly been stored like tins in a larder but now held nothing at all. But we made a go of it. We tramped among livestock and heaps of manure to lay our hands on the slanted monoliths. We squeezed inside one of the cairns with Mum holding her jacket over her shoulders and Dad declaring his fascination at how it might have been, really, if you gave it some thought. And of course the rock carvings, worn down and barely visible at midday, with their cups and rings and stray lines radiating outward. A few looked like dartboards, Peter said. Because he played darts. I spotted a treble clef until I realised it was a trick in the texture, in the cracks and fissures of the rock itself. The only real fun came at the summit of Dunadd when I stepped in the carved footprint used in the first coronation rituals of Scotland and discovered it was a perfect match. Dad dubbed me Violet MacAlpin, conqueror of the Picts and founder of the Kingdom of Alba. Peter dubbed me a royal pain in the arse.

Aaron is the only one I know who could make them mildly interesting. His speculations, his urge to know. His pleasure in the complications. He doesn't expect to solve them, of course, but rather to become satisfied in the effort. Yet he will never be satisfied, even in that. Does he know it yet? Does he know himself?

I hear a tapping of keys, a familiar staccato from his desk across the hall. What on earth could he be typing? I call his name. I wait. I lean out from the bed but see only the scraped file cabinet, the chair plundered from a skip, the lamp with its paper shade burnt by a bulb that gives more heat than light. When we buy this flat I hope we can afford to furnish it properly.

'A friggin' *typewriter*,' Aaron says, jerking his thumb over his shoulder as he comes back through the doorway, his voice flaring with Blue Ridge summer, the gut-level syllables of his younger self. Of course it's still there within him. An ostinato of basic pleasures and straightforward thinking.

I work up a tolerant expression. 'Yes, a typewriter.'

'And the circle jerks.'

'What?'

'Those pages I tacked up. As if I had some great insight into the universe.' He draws a long breath. 'All those years I was putting the cart before the horse. That's one thing Tessa...'

I watch him carefully as he trails off, a flicker of caution in his eyes.

'Anyway,' he says, forcing a shift, 'that typewriter still drops the f's. Oh, and look at *this*.' He goes over to his closet and flicks through the hangars.

'Um, Aaron?'

He pulls out a striped shirt – not one of my favourites – and holds it at arm's length. 'I really used to wear this, didn't I?'

'You don't have the greatest fashion sense, if that's what you mean.'

He gives me a burlesque frown before setting it back.

'I gather you were typing a note to yourself?'

'Hell, no. I just wanted to bang the keys again for old time's sake.'

'But don't you have some advice to offer? A few warnings?' I prop my head on my hand. 'Stock tips, perhaps? There must be some things you'd like to tell yourself.'

'Too many things.'

I try to read the wry gravitas on his face. He must know how he looks, how he sounds. 'All right, then,' I say. 'Fair enough. After all, I suppose it's better this way, isn't it? You certainly wouldn't have left us alone like this. You're the jealous type. Or at least you used to be.'

He pauses to untangle the pronouns, the past and present selves. 'Are you saying you prefer me over him?'

'I'm saying some things improve with age.' I ruffle my hair and allow the sheet to slip.

He eases back, deliberately resisting the temptation, and reaches for his shirt on the floor.

'You haven't told me how it happened,' I say. 'All I know is that it was Halloween night.'

'Sort of,' he says, working his arms into the sleeves. He fastens the buttons in silence.

'Oh dear. Suddenly you're evasive. A while ago you were babbling away about a windstorm and trick-or-treating with our daughter. Tessa. I must have chosen that name. After my gran. And our son, what do we call him?'

He inhales. 'Can we change the subject?'

'Why?'

'I've already told you too much.'

'What difference does it make if you tell me our son's name? You've already warned me about your pottery expert and her clay jugs or whatever it is that you find so attractive. But really, Aaron. You can't start that kind of thing and just *stop*.'

'I told you about Siobhan because it's worth the risk. Now will you drop it, please?'

'Worth what risk?'

He holds up a hand. 'Can you just trust me on this? I have to be careful. I don't know how it all works. What kind of damage I might do. What damage I've already done.'

I roll onto my back. 'Well, unless you murdered someone or robbed a bank on your way here, I don't think you have much to worry about. The only difference is what you've told me. We'll have a daughter and a son. Our daughter will break a lamp. We'll have the flat repainted, presumably after we manage to buy it. Oh goodness, think of the disruption, the great rip in the fabric of the space-time.'

Wrong thing to say. He crouches down and ties his shoelaces with a hard look on his face. What happened to his gleeful nihilism? His urge for existential mischief? All those late-night rhapsodies about geological timescales and the insignificance of the human race? He's taking the wrong track. He's confusing the score with the music, the treble with the bass, the right hand with the left. As if one thing causes the other. Oh, Aaron. That's not how it goes. Let's sequence the motif. Let's try a different key. Let's improvise.

'Are you going to tell her?' I ask.

'You mean –'

'Me. Her. The future Violet. This woman who disapproves of trick-or-treating. Are you going to tell her what's happened between us?'

'I guess I won't need to. She'll already know because…' he gestures at me '…well, you're her. Or you're going to be her.'

'Don't be so sure.'

He gives me an indulgent smile. 'You planning on a severe case of amnesia between now and then?'

'I'm just saying we could be different people.'

'Come on, Vi.'

'Because this is probably a different *place* as well as a different time.'

He opens his mouth, but loses whatever he's going to say next. Then he seems to lift slowly from his moorings. A pulse of sunlight comes into the room, bringing a higher voltage, a renewed circuitry to every surface and texture.

'A separate reality,' he says. 'A parallel universe. Which would mean that whatever happens here…' He shifts his gaze back to me.

I flick my eyebrows at him and stretch out with a feline extravagance.

He comes over for what he probably tells himself is just a kiss, but then his face is buried in my hair and I'm working his shirt off again. He grips me with an almost helpless greed. I have to reach back and brace myself against the headboard, working into the pleasure until we're breathing together and I feel his hands cupping my face as if he's afraid of losing it, sliding down afterward with his forehead pressed to the space between my breasts. I feel him trembling. Then something seizes him and he shoves himself away. A fracture between us like shattered glass.

He dresses himself brusquely, with a flinty edge to his expression, giving his lapels a hard tug. 'I need tools,' he says.

I run the words over, thinking I must have I misheard.

'A hammer,' he adds. 'Or at least a screwdriver. Otherwise I can't go back.'

'Well, you know where they are,' I manage to say. 'Or were. I guess we might move them to a different cupboard by 2006.'

I wait for more – an explanation, a response of some kind – but he finishes dressing in silence, a clamped emotion in his mouth. I watch him through wet eyes. Something is wrong. Not now. Then. In the future.

'What is it?' I ask. 'What's happening to us?'

He leaves the bedroom without replying. I wipe my eyes and listen to the creaking hinges of the cupboard. The rattle of the toolbox. The lid's metallic thud. There's a rustling, a yanking, a scraping inside the closet itself. What could he possibly be doing? And then he repacks everything slowly, with that special care of his, leaving no trace.

No. I won't let it end this way. I'll bring him back. The other Violet and I can share him. What's mine is hers, what's hers is mine. Yes, that's the key. It's how everything falls into place. The sharps, the flats, the accidentals. The intervals and chords. The perfect fifth. As he walks down the hallway his footsteps become the rhythm, my heartbeat the time. The door shuts behind him with a click like a metronome. I can play it now. And it goes like this.

Anne Rouse

Night of the Monkey Puzzle Tree

Green ziggurat, it jigsaws the view
with needle-tipped, serrated boughs,
lizard teeth in out-sized jaws,
haunting the suburban present,
a country beyond accident.

The monkeys triumph, currently.
The Holocene age evolved between
its scissor branches: book and screen,
traffic growling up the ridge,
began under a blackthorn hedge.

Dwindling to whitened clemency,
the slow night ends; its brawlers pale;
each flash of claw has left our sentinel
unmarked and unimpressed; only loftier,
rooted in gore, attempting the hereafter.

Across its jagged workman's weave
outriders of the sun prevail
and now the uneven shadows steal
into the morning's reckoning
through every baffled dream.

It Greens Again

It greens again, as if dressing for a fete.
Gladrags wave, hucksters warble in the copse.
The show's the thing; forget the seedy runners
underground, the last year's rot and weight,

The dance duplicitous: this evening we decide,
as winged replicas bid fretfully to hatch,
and blowsy come-ons veil the angling spores,
like chaste observers that we'll sit outside

– although the glade exhales our oxygen
and we're bound to the self-same waltz
(obdurate ephemera, insisting that clods
transmogrify, according to a cloud-capped vision) –

clocking our native triumph from afar: a headlong
rush into jouissance, tallying abundance
in a cistern of rain, a bush, a bee-hung spire;
twinned at the crooked root, torch singer, and song.

Cyclops in Cythera

We've freed ourselves, friend; neither of us sleeps alone.
Three winters on, this squalling is just weather.
Doves, grey deacons, haver in the eaves.
Torn clouds resume their westering.

Out of the cave that led from you, dear Terror,
I ran seaward as the boulders fell, yards off,
rattling like coins. Your bellowing grew tinny, small;
a dry leaf eddying, the rock-face sealed behind.

I pretended, of course, that you peered after me,
a tower darkening around an eye,
trembling in a haze that ebbed and stained,
Pharos, a lamp for inbound craft to sail by,

until the horizon blinked, and overturned.
Now the trees may swarm, gusts chivvy the bells,
as if our charts or instruments were down;
as if your one-eyed image bleeds, and hovers

– but it's a rose window, this, welling with day,
as every airless chamber overruns.
I lift the latch, lean out and drink the sun,
an absence; a caroling of bells.

Willy Maley

Fifty Shades of Gray:
Empire, Inequality and Empowerment in *Poor Things* (1992)

Alasdair Gray's *Poor Things*, published twenty years ago, is a book that raises questions about class, education, empire, equality, gender and genre that remain pressingly relevant today. What kind of novel is *Poor Things*? To which genre does it belong? Is it postmodern? Postcolonial? Victorian? Gothic? Magic realist? Is it perhaps a polemical postmodernist postcolonial pastiche that can't be pigeonholed or pinned down as easily as I've just tried to do? When Thomas Hardy wrote *Tess of the d'Urbervilles* in 1891, he put, as a subtitle, *A Pure Woman*. That subtitle – 'A Pure Woman' – caused as much consternation as the subject matter of the book itself. Hardy reflected on his choice after the dust had settled on the dustjacket: 'Respecting the sub-title', he wrote, 'I may add that it was appended at the last moment, after reading the final proofs, as being the estimate left in a candid mind of the heroine's character – an estimate that nobody would be likely to dispute. It was disputed more than anything else in the book. *Melius fuerat non scriber*. But there it stands'.[1]

If Thomas Hardy had called Tess a 'poor woman' – a 'poor thing' – rather than a 'pure woman', he might just have got away with it. Purity and poverty don't mix. By suggesting that a woman from a poor background who was raped and hung could be 'pure', Hardy was inviting the outrage of the more conservative elements of Victorian society. Another writer of the time, Henry James, hated *Tess*, not because of Hardy's insistence on his heroine's purity or innocence, but because he thought Hardy's novel was 'chock-full of faults and falsity', as he put it in a letter to Robert Louis Stevenson on 19 March 1892.

Here was a young woman, 'a pure woman', in Hardy's subtitle, used and abused, before being finally dispatched to the gallows, a victim of her gender. In his own fiction, Henry James preferred women to affront their destinies, to go against the grain of a culture that conspired to defeat or disappoint them. One way of approaching *Poor Things* is to see it as part of a tradition that would include Maisie in Henry James's *What Maisie Knew*, as well as Isobel Archer in *Portrait of a Lady*, Caroline Meeber in Theodore Dreiser's *Sister Carrie*, Molly Bloom in James Joyce's *Ulysses*, and more recently the title character in Alan Warner's *Morvern Callar*, all male creations of female characters who take their destinies into their own hands. Or we can see her as the artist figure favoured by Virginia Woolf and by Oscar Wilde. Detachment, observation, and, coming back to Joyce, renunciation. Muriel Spark also despised the literature of pity, of sentiment. Spark knew that the reader fed on pity grew fat and inert:

> He has undergone the experience of pity for the underdog. Salt tears have gone bowling down his cheeks. He has had a good dinner. He is absolved, he sleeps well. He rises refreshed, more determined than ever to be the overdog. And there is always, too, the man who finds the heroic role of the victim so appealing that he'll never depart from it. I suggest that wherever there is a cult of the victim, such being human nature, there will be an obliging cult of twenty equivalent victimisers.[2]

Janice Galloway has singled Alasdair Gray out for praise for his enlightened views on gender:

> Gray's writing… is informed by a democratic urge that does not sell women short: he knows our version of the story is different, possibly even opposed, yet of equal force… Gray's writing not only knows that women experience, feel, and often think differently, it seems to be filled with a regret for that fact, and in this way, Woman – the female principal – exists in Gray's writing the way she exists in no other current male writer's work.[3]

Alasdair Gray's *Poor Things*, if looked at as a late Victorian morality tale – which is certainly what, on one level, it masquerades as – can be seen as part of a tradition in which male authors choose women as their chief protagonists. Often these are rescue narratives, where a woman is rescued by a supportive male figure. Like Dostoevsky in *Notes From Underground* (published in Russian in 1864, translated into English in 1918), in *Poor Things* Gray plays subversively with the idea of the rescued female narrative, interrogating the idea of a male maker or savior who redeems a 'fallen' woman (literally fallen in the river in this case). In fact, you could say that *Poor Things* contains two stories, one about a victim, and the other about a victor (Godwin Baxter puns on Victoria's name meaning 'victory' – 'Bella Victoria, you Beautiful Victory'). There is, on the one hand, the story of a young woman who is driven to despair and suicide by a middle-class and male-dominated culture, and, on the other hand, there is the story of another woman – the same woman, as it turns out – who gains knowledge through experience and insight, and thus becomes a worldly-wise and responsible citizen.

The story of Victoria Hattersley, in her passage from slums to suicide, might have pleased Thomas Hardy. And there was a kind of realism to it. (The Ophelia Syndrome, at least according to Godwin Baxter, was a reality for many young women.) The story of her alter ego, Bella Baxter or Victoria McCandless, might have pleased Henry James, as an instance of what he would have regarded as a triumph of the spirit or the will over circumstances or fate.

Most novels are Frankenstein fabrications, made up of lots of different bits and pieces of text, social commentary, philosophical musing, travel writing and so on. Most of the time we can't see the joins – we're not supposed to – but there are certain writers who want us to see the bones beneath the skin, the working out behind the fictional formulae, who want us to know that a novel is a text made up of other texts. Are such writers 'postmodernist'? And are labels like postmodernism appropriate means of pigeonholing or pinning down a literary text?

Alasdair Gray has himself expressed scepticism about the label 'postmodernist' being attached to his work, partly because he thinks of it as a new-fangled term, and he sees himself as an old-fashioned writer who belongs firmly within a literary tradition in which writers are constantly experimenting with form at the same time as they are responding to their immediate social worlds. In an interview, Gray says:

> I don't think I am [a Postmodernist]. To me postmodernism is a school of
> criticism, not a school of writing. I think I'm an old-fashioned modernist

like James Joyce or Laurence Sterne – we've been around for a very long time… The business of writers and their work addressing the world that's around them and the assumption that the great writers of the past carefully separated their immediate politics from the art form they created, is mainly based on our ignorance of the past. To say that the notion of the writer putting themselves as a character into the story they are telling is in any way postmodern, I think, is hilarious.[4]

And it's true that if one were to argue that Gray's use of critical notes and commentary in his texts, for example, were postmodern, then Edmund Spenser's *Shepheardes Calendar*, published four hundred years earlier, would be postmodern too, as would T.S. Eliot's *The Waste Land*. Yet despite the protests of the author, critics persist in seeing Gray's work in terms of 'postmodernism'. What does it mean? Well, according to Gray, one of the signs of postmodernism was that an author dipped into a pool of previous writing, quite self-consciously. Other ingredients include undecidability, open-endedness, and inconclusiveness. Derek Attridge puts it like this:

> Postmodernism's commerce between elite and popular culture, its amalgamation of pastiche and quotation, its games with self-referentiality, its preference for mixed and open forms, its courting of the arbitrary and the random, its resistance to the 'serious' or the 'natural': all these features of recent art in a variety of media could be thought of as producing not the sense of necessary cohesion that characterises most modernist and pre-modernist art, but a sense of the constantly renewed possibility of connection, in which the history and situation of each interpreter provides one set of elements in the network of potentialities. Rather than art which exploits its culture in an attempt to transcend it, it is an art which celebrates its embeddedness in that culture, and remains open to changes within it. Among the many writers in English one might think of in connection with such an art are John Ashbery, Donald Barthelme, Angela Carter, Alasdair Gray, Thomas Pynchon, and Salman Rushdie.[5]

In an early essay on *Poor Things*, Philip Hobsbaum viewed Gray's novel as postmodern precisely because it is hard for the reader to choose between the two narratives it offers, the two versions of the story it presents:

There can be no determined conclusion. What the reader looks at is a distinctively post-modernist novel… Both interpretations are possible: *Poor Things* A and *Poor Things* B are able to co-exist within the same text. But the text leaves us poised between the alternatives. The novel is either (A) about a woman remade by a doctor of genius or (B) about a woman rescued by a doctor of considerable talent.[6]

Now, you could argue that *Poor Things* offers not just two perspectives, and that the choice between being remade or rescued is pretty limited. Are we looking at *The Bride of Frankenstein* or *Pretty Woman* here? In Gray's novel, we actually get several different texts. There's an Introduction by Alasdair Gray, calling himself the editor of a text that has come into his hands, a 'found text' entitled *Episodes from the Early Life of a Scottish Public Health Officer* allegedly by one Archibald McCandless. This text is broken up again by two long letters, one from Bella Baxter, a woman who is supposed to have been made or remade by Godwin Baxter, and one from Duncan Wedderburn, the man with whom she eloped and traveled to Europe and Africa. The McCandless text – not all of which is by McCandless – is followed by 'A letter about the book to a grand- or great grandchild by "Victoria" McCandless M.D. [also known as Bella Baxter].' In this section, the woman who is the subject of the narrative by Archibald McCandless, his wife, tells her side of the story, directly contradicting her late husband's version of events. The final text consists of 'CHAPTER NOTES, HISTORICAL AND CRITICAL', by Alasdair Gray. At the very end, there are the illustrations that appear throughout the book, portraits and maps, forming another text, and telling another story, about the body and the city. As well as being a postmodern novel – if it is one – and a neo-Victorian novel – *Poor Things* is also a Scottish novel and a socialist one.

In one of the most interesting essays on Gray – all the more interesting for being somewhat unsympathetic – Alison Lumsden takes issue with the critical consensus that sees Gray's writing as being both formally innovative and politically committed. Lumsden seems to think that these two views of Gray's writing don't fit together very well, that the socially engaged rhetoric, especially when it is specific to Scotland, or even Glasgow, somehow compromises or undermines the literary experimentation. Lumsden has problems with both the Scottish dimensions of Gray's writing and its socialist stance. She takes issue with what she sees as a distinct moral strand in Gray's work:

While Gray has claimed that it is the business of the novelist to avoid the role of moralist, this impulse in his fiction seems an undeniably didactic reflex; a reluctance to leave his fictions *free* in some more ambiguous area where the reader may or may not read some direct social issues (most frequently the state of Scotland, or even more parochially Glasgow) into them.[7]

Like Bella and her Creator, the text should be free to make its own way in the world without its author anxiously watching over it. Now, Lumsden's essay was written before *Poor Things* was published – it's mainly concerned with Gray's earlier novel, *Lanark* (1981) – but you can see how her criticisms could be applied to this novel. Lumsden is clearly unhappy with Gray's tendency to harp on about Scotland:

> Again, metaphoric expansiveness is narrowed down to the specific, as the author ensures that his own opinions on the state of Scotland will form part of the structure of the work of fiction. These opinions surely serve only to *contain* the fictional whole, limiting its field of reference and the wider thematic impulses which it has achieved.[8]

Lumsden accuses Gray of 'cutting his critique to the size of a parochial polemic'. She sees this strategy of banging the drum for Glasgow and Scotland as somehow limiting Gray's wider appeal.

Lumsden's last point about Gray is that he tends to pre-empt criticism of his work by incorporating critical commentary into his fiction, such as epilogues and other 'critic fodder'. According to Lumsden:

> it is possible to read such material in terms of critique, seeing it as an attempt to short-circuit the inevitable containment of the radicalism of fictional writing by critical commentary. However, again it seems important at least to suggest that by this strategy Gray may only be timidly seeking to contain responses to his fiction, 'drawing the poison' of potential critical debate so that it can only take place within the reflexively pre-emptive terms that Gray has prescribed for it, thus again stifling rather than supporting any real radicalism in his fiction.[9]

Now, the idea that Gray as a writer is limiting the role of the critic – and the role of the reader, since every reader is a critic – by surrounding his own fiction with the guard rail of his own criticism might be missing the point, which is that Gray is a critic too, and a very good one.

However, Lumsden's four criticisms of Gray are I think important when it comes to seeing how *Poor Things* operates. Just to recap: First, Lumsden sees an inconsistency between formal experimentation and social and political content, between text and ideology, between what she actually calls 'innovation' on the one hand, and 'reaction' on the other. Secondly, she sees a contradiction in Gray's remark that the writer shouldn't be a moralist and the presence of a strong moral strand within his work. In other words, Gray can't resist the very didacticism, the preaching, that he has remarked upon elsewhere as inappropriate for fiction. Thirdly, Lumsden considers Gray's focus on Scottish and Glaswegian issues to be limiting. You can't be local or national and at the same time international or universal. Fourth and finally, Gray's use of criticism within his fiction – the editorial apparatus, the mock-scholarship – is intended to ward off criticism, Lumsden argues, rather than encourage it – a decoy rather than a doorway.

According to Randall Stevenson, 'Lumsden argues persuasively that Gray's postmodernism is so derivative, 'clumsily-handled', and formulaic as to annul most of the liberating unconventionality once promised by postmodernist techniques'.[10] Postmodernism – ugly, fashionable, jargon-ridden word that it is – is being used by critics as a way of thinking chiefly about form. But might there be a way of classifying Gray's work that allows both for its innovative form and its political content? The whole postmodern angle, especially when obsessed by form, may turn out to be a bit of a dead-end. *Poor Things* is about the making of a Scottish socialist feminist. Why should that disqualify it from being postmodernist?

Another way of thinking about Gray's work comes from the German critic H. Gustav Klaus, who is interested in representations of working-class culture. Rather than seeing Gray as a postmodern author who lets himself and his readers down by indulging in 'parochial polemic', Klaus takes the context of Gray's writing seriously, seeing in Gray's socialist polemics a Scottish national or 'postcolonial' response to English or British imperialism. According to Klaus: 'This focus on the working class and the concomitant attack on middle-class values […] is by no means a Scottish peculiarity, but widespread in what goes under the name of 'New Literatures in English', resulting as it does from the association of the native ruling elite with the colonisers'.[11] Thus instead of comparing Gray with other British or English or American 'postmodern' writers, Klaus would want to see Gray in the light of, say, African writers. Gray would come closer, then, to Chinua Achebe, or Ben Okri, than to Martin Amis. The postcolonial approach, which takes the national and political dimensions of the novel seriously, may actually be more useful when it comes to thinking about Alasdair Gray's fiction than a postmodern position that separates form and content.

So much for the critics, what about the text? *Poor Things* is a book about self-fashioning and social mobility, about making it, about making yourself and others, and about the power of making that comes from experience and education, from medical science, and from creation or imagination. Right from the very beginning, the author is on the make. 'Make something of yourself with it', says McCandless's mother to her son, on giving him her life savings. 'I told her I would make myself a doctor', says McCandless, on accepting the money.[12]

When McCandless goes to Glasgow University, as the son of a farmer from the Borders, he finds it hard to fit in with his fellow students. A professor tells him that he must reform himself, change his appearance:

'Mr. McCandless, in a just world I could predict a brilliant future for you, but not in this one, unless you make some changes […] unless you acquire a touch of smooth lordliness or easy-going humour no patient will trust you, other doctors will shun you […] If you cannot afford a good coat from a good tailor, search for one that fits you among forfeited pledges in the better pawnshops. Sleep with your trousers neatly folded between two boards under your mattress. If you cannot change your linen every day at least contrive to attach a freshly starched collar to your shirt. Attend conversaziones and smoking-concerts arranged by the class you are studying to join – you will not find us a bad set of people, and will gradually fit in by a process of instinctive imitation'. (pp. 10–11)

Instinctive imitation – or mimicry, to use a term favoured by postcolonial critic Homi Bhabha – is one way of passing for middle class or authoritative. Sadly, it is not just his appearance but also his accent that gives McCandless away. He is a bit of a misfit because of the way he speaks. Class, even when it's invisible (unlike gender or race) is seldom inaudible. A fellow student, after hearing McCandless speak out at a lecture, says:

> 'I'm sorry we laughed McCandless, but to hear you steadily quoting Comte and Huxley and Haeckel in your broad Border dialect was like hearing the Queen opening parliament in the voice of a Cockney costermonger'. (p. 16)

McCandless isn't very happy about being made to feel foolish because he appears less refined than his fellow students, and part of his story is the story of an outsider, someone who doesn't feel at home, chiefly because of his standing in the social order. McCandless is a bit of a malcontent, and that governs the way he reads or writes his wife's story. In his account, she is a woman moulded by men, who comes to loathe inequality and suffering. In her version it is social envy that structures her husband's worldview.

In McCandless's narrative, Godwin Baxter – God for short – revives a pregnant woman who has committed suicide by throwing herself into the River Clyde. He brings her back to life by taking the brain of her baby and transplanting it into the mother's head. Baxter, as well as being a doctor, is a social reformer and champion of women's rights. He tells McCandless: 'Every year hundreds of young women drown themselves because of the poverty and prejudices of our damnably unfair society' (p. 33). There are shades of Jonathan Swift here and *A Modest Proposal*. Baxter does not wish 'Bella', the woman he has (re)invented, to know that she is his creation: 'It would cast a shadow upon her life to learn that she is a surgical fabrication' (p. 35).

All of the characters in *Poor Things* tell their stories at some point in terms of their interpretation of a particular piece of literature, in a kind of cannibalisation of the canon. Embedded in the novel are readings of a familiar corpus of texts, containing a kind of criticism, often eccentric and oblique. In Godwin Baxter's case, his story is his reading of *Hamlet*, and in particular of Ophelia's role, and his desire to save a woman who is a victim of 'our damnably unfair society'. The 'Ophelia Complex' obsesses Baxter, and with it sympathy for a woman wronged:

> 'I read the miserable story of the play in which she was the one true loving soul. It obviously described the spread of an epidemic brain fever which,

like typhoid, was perhaps caused by seeping from the palace graveyard into the Elsinore water supply. From an inconspicuous start among sentries on the battlements the infection spread through the prince, king, prime minister and courtiers causing hallucinations, logomania and paranoia resulting in insane suspicions and murderous impulses. I imagined myself entering the palace quite early in the drama with all the executive powers of an efficient public health officer. The main carriers of the disease (Claudius, Polonius and the obviously incurable Hamlet) would be quarantined in separate wards. A fresh water supply and efficient modern plumbing would soon set the Danish state right and Ophelia, seeing this gruff Scottish doctor pointing her people toward a clean and healthy future, would be powerless to withhold her love.' (pp. 39–40)

Bella reads her story in terms of another work of fiction, Emily Brontë's *Wuthering Heights*. Speaking to Mr McCandless of her relationship with Godwin Baxter, her creator, she says:

> 'most folk think God and me a very gothic couple. They are wrong. At heart we are ordinary farmers like Cathy and Heathcliff in *Wuthering Heights* by one of those Brontës [...] Heathcliff and Cathy belong to a farming family and he loves her because they've been together and played together almost forever and she likes him a lot but finds Edgar more lovable and marries him because he is outside the family. Then Heathcliff goes daft. I hope Baxter won't.' (p. 51)

These madmen, Hamlet and Heathcliff, driven by frustrated ambition, are what women don't want. They need treatment. While they're looking up, others are looking down.

Elsewhere, Duncan Wedderburn alludes to productions of Goethe's *Faust* and Goldsmith's *She Stoops to Conquer* at the Glasgow Theatre Royal in order to illustrate his predicament as the respectable middle class man who sells his soul to 'women of the servant class'.

Baxter's mission in recreating Bella is to have her see how society works. He does this by allowing her to go out into the world and learn from what she sees. The message of Gray's novel is quite similar to the message of Henry James's fiction. James believed that literature was a very good teacher. Formal education of the type provided by schools and universities was designed to make students subservient. Experience and observation, by contrast, can liberate. Bella describes her own miseducation in these terms: '*Mother had taught me to be a working man's domestic slave; the nuns taught me to be a rich man's domestic toy*' (pp. 258–59; italics in original).

The first question that arises on reading *Poor Things* concerns the title. The title that the editor (Alasdair Gray) chooses to give to Archibald McCandless's account (and his wife's refutation of it) is arguably the least convincing aspect of the introduction. Gray says simply:

> I have […] insisted on renaming the whole book POOR THINGS. Things are often mentioned in the story and every single character (apart from Mrs. Dinwiddie and two of the General's parasites) is called poor or call themselves that sometime or other. (p. xiii)

It seems a poor excuse for a title. A better one might have been 'The Miseducation of Victoria Hattersley'. But if we're stuck with *Poor Things* we might as well ask: Who or what are the *poor things* of the title?

Duncan Wedderburn's story is one of temptation and ruin, but when McCandless shows some sympathy for his rival's plight, Baxter says:

> 'Why worry about Wedderburn, McCandless? He is a middle-class male in the prime of life with legal training, a secure home and three supportive females. Think of your fiancée, the attractive woman with the three-year old brain he has left penniless in Paris. Do you not fear for her?'
>
> 'No, [replies McCandless] with all his advantages Wedderburn is a poor creature. Bell is not.' (p. 99)

McCandless, in saying that Wedderburn, the middle-class professional male, is a 'poor creature', has hit on something. He has hit on another meaning of the word 'poor'. Poor here doesn't mean badly off financially, but deserving of sympathy, weak, lacking agency. Bella, though poor in terms of social background, is not poor in this sense. Later, Godwin's dying wish is that Bella will look after his 'poor lonely leaderless dogs' (p. 271).

One of the characters who convinces Bella Baxter that she must work to make the world a better place is Dr Hooker, an American white supremacist.

His theory of racial purity sickens her and makes her want to fight inequality, so rather than settle down with Harry Astley she chooses socialism over selfishness:

> *I felt for the first time who [Harry Astley] really is – a tortured little boy who hates cruelty as much as I do but thinks himself a strong man because he can pretend to like it. He is as poor and desperate as my lost daughter, but only inside. Outside he is perfectly comfortable. Everyone should have a cosy shell round them, a good coat with money in the pockets. I must become a Socialist.* (p. 164)

Once again, purity and poverty are at issue. The turning point for Bella comes with a trip to Egypt, to Alexandria – which the British bombarded from the sea in 1882 – where she sees naked and blind children begging from wealthy tourists. She is very distraught by this sight, and tries to help two of the children, but is told by her companions, Mr Astley and Dr Hooker, that she can do no good:

> *YOU CAN DO NO GOOD bellowed Dr. Hooker nobody had ever cursed me and insulted me like that before how could he say that to me who like all of us is good right through to the backbone I CAN DO NO GOOD? I cried hardly believing I had heard such a vile suggestion but Mr. Astley said distinctly none at all so I tried to scream like you once screamed God since I wanted to make the whole world faint but Harry Astley clapped his hand over my mouth O the sheer joy of feeling my teeth sink in.* (p. 174)

Archibald McCandless's narrative is the tale of a woman who was brought back to life by a man. Bella's own narrative, after she has reverted to her original name, Victoria, and married McCandless, goes against her husband's account. For Victoria McCandless the real story, her story, not his story, is that of a woman who was raised to be an aristocrat's plaything. She was going to be operated on for 'erotomania' by a Glasgow doctor. The doctor turned out to be more sympathetic to her case than her husband. She then fled to Glasgow to be with that doctor, Godwin Baxter, but was rejected by him, and so married a friend of his, when both of them really loved 'God'. Victoria McCandless/Bella Baxter gives the reader a choice similar to the one offered by Philip Hobsbaum, between two conflicting interpretations of the text:

You, dear reader, have now two accounts to choose between and there can be no doubt which is most probable. My second husband's story positively stinks of all that was morbid in that most morbid of centuries, the nineteenth… Ever since reading this infernal parody of my life-story I have been asking, WHY DID ARCHIE WRITE IT? I am now able to post this letter to posterity because I have at last found an answer.

As locomotive engines are driven by pressurised steam, so the mind of Archibald McCandless was driven by carefully hidden envy. His good fortune in later life never stopped him being at heart just 'a poor bastard bairn'. The envy the poor and exploited feel toward the wealthy is a good thing if it works toward reforming this unfairly ordered nation […] Unluckily my Archie envied the only two people he loved, the only two who could tolerate him. He envied God for having a famous father and tender, loving mother. He resented my wealthy father, convent education and famous first husband, resented my superior social graces. (pp. 272–73)

Once more we are back with class, and with the way in which gender is used by a male author or narrator in order to say something about social injustice that might otherwise be too difficult to say. In fact, having taken what could be read as an empowered position as a woman with regard to her dead husband's version of events, Victoria McCandless goes on to indulge in exactly the kind of social polemic that Godwin Baxter, Archibald McCandless and Alasdair Gray are all so fond of:

But I have no time to go through every page separating fact from fiction. If you ignore what contradicts common sense and this letter you will find that this book records some actual events during a dismal era. As I said before, to my nostrils the book stinks of Victorianism. It is as sham-gothic as the Scott Monument, Glasgow University, St. Pancras Station and the Houses of Parliament. I hate such structures. Their useless over-ornamentation was paid for out of needlessly high profits: profits squeezed from the stunted lives of children, women and men working more than twelve hours a day, six days a week in NEEDLESSLY filthy factories; for by the nineteenth century we had the knowledge to make things cleanly. We did not use it. The huge profits of the owning classes were too sacred to be questioned. To me this book stinks as the interior of a poor woman's crinoline must have stunk after a cheap weekend railway excursion to the Crystal Palace. I realise I am taking it too seriously, but I am thankful to have survived into the twentieth century. (pp. 274–75)

As long as she survived she could speak for herself, but one of the last notes supplied by Alasdair Gray as editor reads:

> Dr. Victoria McCandless was found dead of a cerebral stroke on the 3rd December 1946. Reckoning from the birth of her brain in the Humane Society mortuary on Glasgow Green, 18th February 1880, she was exactly sixty-six years, forty weeks and four days old. Reckoning from the birth of her body in a Manchester slum in 1854, she was ninety-two. (p. 317)

Thus the 'editor', Alasdair Gray, is complicit with Archibald McCandless's version of events, the one that attributes the ridge on his wife's skull, not to a knock on the head she got from her father, but to an operation carried out by Godwin Baxter to save her life and that of her child.

According to Henry James – and, who knows, this might make him a postmodernist – 'the novel is history'.[13] Writing over a hundred years ago, James argued that novels ought to grow up, so that they could address their readers – increasingly female, increasingly disinclined to marry – and stop being patronising or needlessly and inappropriately romantic. It remains for readers of all ages, sexes and classes to argue whether Alasdair Gray's *Poor Things* is just another example of the male author's effort to create a strong woman who can articulate the injustice of class differences more overtly than he can, like a good ventriloquist's dummy, or whether it is a more radical attempt to show that class and gender inequalities are tied up together in a knot. Bella Baxter, in one of the book's illustrations, is depicted as 'Bella Caledonia' or Beautiful Scotland (p. 45). This plays upon the conventional stereotype of the nation as female, like Ireland's Cathleen Ni Houlihan. But there is also, in Godwin Baxter's plea that Bella lead his 'poor dogs', an appeal to the woman as a provider of political leadership. In *A History Maker*, Gray subscribes to a 'mild matriarchy' as a desirable form of government.[14] I grew up with five older sisters – big sisters – and I can heartily recommend a severe matriarchy. But enough about me – no, seriously! Let's leave the last word to God... I mean Gray:

> That is what comes of being praised or condemned as a postmodernist. It is as bad as being praised or condemned as an exponent of Marxist dialectic. I told you *Poor Things* would please academics and non-university

folk because I enjoyed writing it so much I was sure many would like reading it. It contained no original devices at all. The editor's introduction of long lost narrative was in *The Master of Ballantrae*. That book, as well as *The Moonstone* and *Frankenstein*, is told by a narrator who quotes long narratives by other people, many of them letters. But why explain where I got the tried and true ideas for constructing the *Poor Things* automobile? I want the reader to enjoy driving it.[15]

1. Thomas Hardy, Preface to *Tess of the d'Urbervilles: A Pure Woman Faithfully Presented* [1891], March 1912 (London and New York: Harper & Brothers Publishers, 1920), pp. xx–xxi.

2. Muriel Spark, 'The Desegregation of Art', from 'Muriel Spark on Herself and Her Art', in Joseph Hynes (ed.), *Critical Essays on Muriel Spark* (New York: G.K. Hall, 1992), p. 35.

3. Janice Galloway, 'Reading Alasdair Gray', *Context* 7 (2001), http://www.dalkeyarchive.com/book/?GCOI=15647100550300&fa=customcontent&extrasfile=A1261DEF-B0D0-B086-B69DA9EF962D9E76.html, accessed 8 October 2012.

4. Alasdair Gray, 'An Old-Fashioned Modernist: Alasdair Gray talks to Joe McAvoy', *Cencrastus* 61 (1998), p. 7.

5. Derek Attridge, *Joyce Effects: On Language, Theory, and History* (Cambridge: Cambridge University Press, 2000), p.119.

6. Philip Hobsbaum, 'Unreliable Narrators: *Poor Things* and its Paradigms', *The Glasgow Review* 3 (1995), p. 46.

7. Alison Lumsden, 'Innovation and Reaction in the Fiction of Alasdair Gray', in Gavin Wallace and Randall Stevenson (eds.), *The Scottish Novel Since the Seventies* (Edinburgh: Edinburgh University Press, 1993), p. 122.

8. Lumsden, 'Innovation and Reaction in the Fiction of Alasdair Gray', p. 122.

9. Lumsden, 'Innovation and Reaction in the Fiction of Alasdair Gray', p. 123.

10. Randall Stevenson, 'A Postmodern Scotland?', in Gerard Carruthers, David Goldie and Alastair Renfrew (eds.), *Beyond Scotland: New Contexts for Twentieth-Century Scottish Literature* (Amsterdam and New York: Rodopi, 2004), p. 215, citing Lumsden 1993, p. 119.

11. H. Gustav Klaus, '1984 Glasgow: Alasdair Gray, Tom Leonard, James Kelman',

Etudes Ecossaises (Grenoble), 2 (1993), p. 31.

12. Alasdair Gray, *Poor Things: Episodes from the Early Life of Archibald McCandless, M. D. Scottish Public Health Officer, edited by Alasdair Gray* (London: Bloomsbury, 1992; Penguin, 1993), p. 9. Further references to Gray's novel will be by page number in the text.

13. Henry James, 'The Art of Fiction (1884)', in Morris Shapiro (ed.), *Henry James: Selected Literary Criticism* (London: Peregrine, 1988), p. 80.

14. Alasdair Gray, *A History Maker* (Edinburgh: Canongate, 1994), p. 189.

15. Mark Axelrod, 'An Epistolary Interview, Mostly With Alasdair Gray', *Review of Contemporary Fiction* 15, 2 (1995), p. 115.

Kevin Cahill

Goose-Tip Pen

i.m. Ivor Gurney

When the blurred sorrel
in his skull-cap

got arranged
like a crop circle

one guessed it stood
at ZX91616

on the grid reference;
a dizzying height

of cow's shit
and human blood,

stood between Wotton-under-Edge
and Fauquissart;

after he was beside himself
and fell

over and could not get up
at Stone House

the singing stopped,
the eating stopped,

the sleeping stopped,
the piano stopped,

the sunshine stopped,
the poetry   stayed   sat up late

on knolls
at Cotswolds

snowking up lots
of whatnot

x geum like a hospital,
and bog rose, elfwort,

haresfoot
on the verge…he could crush

the mayflowers while the shells,
stroked ping-pong balls

and coughed blood
choked him up…all his lanes

lovers' lanes: arbored over
with nocturnes

and pussy-willows – small boats
on the blue, and folk

following their fingers along
the same map that Gurney used:

stopping just at that laminated spot
of grass his thumb rested on,

the whole body allowed in.

The Syzygy

Once you realise the bust-up
of both sexes resides
within you and you are kind of
shining like electrodes, then the fingers
spark at each pole – the nerves sparking –
the room is a foment of sperm
and perfume.
                    It clears up why
standing in the camisole
and your face floral with ringlets
you feel like a king…or why you feel the wings
sticking in your back
are not actually angel's wings.

Brian McCabe

Rope

I try to keep myself in shape. Some kind of shape. I'm not a fanatic or anything. The boxing's all behind me, I gave all that up years ago, but I still do the exercises – the isometrics, the running, the skipping. I still like to do a bit of rope. My rope's quite heavy, because I oil it with cooking oil. It's something they got us to do in the early days – only then we used lard. The trainers said it kept the rope slick, and over time it made the rope heavier and added to the exercise. I don't know if any of it is true, but we all did it because they told us to. Maybe it was just a way of getting us to look after the things we used, like the way they got us to rub some kind of saddle soap into our gloves to stop the leather from cracking and drying out. It was like getting soldiers to clean their rifles.

I never went in for weights much, but when I went to the gym I used to do some just to keep the pecs from going soft. Plus, I miss the rowing machine and the treadmill. I could do a good few miles on the treadmill no bother, that doesn't feel like exercise to me. That's relaxation, where I come from. If it's a real run I want, I do it outside. You don't need a gym for that. To be honest, I don't really need the gym for the kind of exercises I do. But I sometimes miss it, because I like being with other folk who're doing the same. Plus, I suppose I've spent a lot of my life in gyms and it's just a kind of habit. Folk don't usually think I'm over fifty. I can pass for forty, no bother at all. I'm still fit. Fit as a butcher's dog, as Ernie, my trainer used to say about me. I dress okay – nothing fancy, but I like to look presentable, not like some men my age, with the washed-out t-shirt and the gut hanging over the waistline of the baggy jeans and the beat-up trainers. Maybe I'll start going to the gym again, get a season ticket. Plus, it's the only place somebody like me might have a slim chance of meeting somebody the same age, or with any luck a bit younger, of the opposite sex.

I met Sylvia there – where else could I have met a woman like that? I'll tell you: nowhere. We don't live in the same part of the town. She lives in a big place up in the Grange. I live in a one-bedroom flat. We don't go to the same kind of shops – and I'm not just talking about clothes shops or department stores. I'm talking about food shops. She goes to Waitrose or Marks and Spencer's and buys all kinds of gourmet food. I go to Iceland, Lidls. She tried me with a couple of things early on, when I first started going back to her place after the gym. Chicken breast in some kind of wine sauce. Salmon wrapped in pastry like a parcel. Asparagus with lemon juice and mayonnaise. I ate it all, of course. On my kind of income – I work as a bouncer – you don't turn down free food. Then one day she asked me what I'd like best, so I told her: steak and fried onions, a couple of fried eggs, maybe a fried tomato, some chips, with a couple of slices of bread and butter on the side. I got the feeling she wasn't a great cook, but she could fry a steak just the way I like it, nearly black on the outside but still with a bit of blood on the inside. So she started to make that for me every time. I'll tell you, I was eating like a king up at her place every Friday afternoon. Sometimes I wondered if her husband wouldn't smell it in the kitchen when he got back from work, the smell of frying. I asked her about it once and she said he had no sense of smell. I don't really understand that. Even animals have a sense of smell. In fact, they have a much better sense of smell than us. I've got a cat called Ringo. I didn't call him that because I'm a Beatles fan, although I grew up with all that stuff like a lot of folk my age. I called him Ringo because he's got these markings, rings on his tail and round his body, that look like rings. In fact, they don't just look like rings, they are rings. He was a stray I took in, and now he's company for me. He likes to sit beside me on my couch when I'm watching the boxing on TV. I like to think he enjoys the boxing as well, but I'm sure that's just me being stupid like I've always been. Anyway, Ringo keeps me company. And I feed him on raw liver. And when I come back from the butcher's with that bag of raw liver in my pocket, he can smell it as soon as I come in the door. And if I open the window in the kitchen at night, he jumps up on the windowsill and crouches down to get his nose close to the opening, and I can see his nostrils working. He can identify any living thing in the back green through smell, even an insect. I know that because I've seen Ringo catching an insect as soon as it flies in range of the window. And I think I've got a pretty good sense of smell myself. I know what fear smells like, and I know the smell of victory and defeat in the ring. They are actually quite similar when I think about it. Maybe it's the same smell of blood and sweat and the people – I mean the crowd who're watching – but to one it's the smell of victory and to the other it's the smell of defeat. So it's the same smell but it smells different, depending on if you're winning or losing.

Sylvia only went to the gym on Fridays. I was doing a bit of rope the first time I saw her. She came in wearing a shiny purple leotard, fancy white trainers and black legwarmers. She had a good solid tan – probably from a tanning place, I thought at the time, but it turned out she'd just been on holiday in Spain. Long auburn hair, dyed with a couple of pink streaks. Big green eyes, not too heavy on the mascara. Dangly earrings and a couple of gold chains around her neck. Also, a little gold chain around her ankle. The way she walked reminded me of a skittish horse – long legs and sort of like her feet were still trying to decide where to take her. She was in pretty good shape for her age, she just needed to work on it a bit – like me. I could see where she was coming from. She could probably see where I was coming from as well. Anyway, when she came in I was doing a bit of rope, as I said. I suppose it's not something folk do much in the gym these days, but for me it's force of habit. For me, a workout isn't complete without doing a bit of rope. Anyway, she saw me and stopped to watch. Gave me a big smile. Then she said something I didn't hear, some kind of rhyme. It was a skipping rhyme she remembered from when she was a kid, she told me later.

So I thought, seconds out, ding dong, here we go again. She had a bit of a workout, not much of a workout, but enough for me to get an eyeful of all her bits and pieces moving together. It was enough to get my juices flowing, I'll tell you. So when I saw her going to take a shower, I did the same. It took her a lot longer to shower than me, so I bought a tea and hung about at the drinks machine, then when I saw her at the mirrors, drying her hair, I threw my empty cup in the bin and went over to join her and started combing my own hair.

'Fancy a coffee?' I asked. I'm not too hot on the chat-up lines.

She brushed the hair away from her face and gave me a steady look with those big green eyes of hers.

'I thought you just had one,' she said. She had me there – but it meant she'd been watching me.

'It was tea,' I said. 'It wasn't that good.'

I screwed up my face to show how bad the tea had been.

'Ok, coffee then.'

'Great. Where do you fancy?'

I was trying to think of a nice café nearby, not the kind of greasy spoon I'd usually go to.

She took a lipstick out of her bag and began to touch up her lips.

'I'll think of somewhere.'

'Great.'

'You a boxer, yeah?'

I smiled. 'Used to be.'

'Thought so by the way you skip.'

I took that as some kind of compliment.

'Just amateur, like. Nearly turned pro once but then I got a couple of injuries and had to stay away from it for a while. By the time I'd got back to it, I was that bit older, things had moved on. So I just went on in the amateur circuit… then I sort of lost interest. Won a couple of medals, kind of thing…'

I felt like I was talking too much. When I'm nervous, I'm either tongue-tied or my mouth runs away with me.

'Good for you,' she said, clipping the lipstick shut and throwing it in her bag. 'Ok, let's go.'

I thought we'd go to a café, but she took me back to her place. Her place was in walking distance of the gym, but she had her car – a tidy little Mini Cooper. 'It's just for tootling about the town,' she told me, then drove me to her place.

We never had the coffee. As soon as we're in the door, she's all over me like a rash. I don't even have time to put down my duffel bag and she's got me up against the door and we're doing tongues and our hands are all over each other. I thought we were going to do it there and then, but after a while she slips the bag off my shoulder, opens it and takes out my rope and she loops it round my neck and laughs.

Then she leads me, like a dog on a leash, up the stairs to the bedroom and the king-size bed.

Then I found out what the rope was for. She liked to be tied to the bed.

Got me to use the rope for her hands, and gave me a couple of long scarves for her feet. It was a bit weird, like, but I wasn't complaining.

Of course, she had a husband. He was called Alasdair and he was a dentist. Not an ordinary dentist, an orthodontist. Must have made a few bob at it, judging from the place. She'd been an air hostess until she gave it up to look after their kids – they had two boys who'd left home, both at college. So there I was, banging her in her marital bed, while Alasdair was out fixing people's teeth. That bothered me a bit. Not that I was worried about him coming home early and throwing me out of the window – I saw photographs of the guy around the house, and he didn't look the type to throw anybody or anything out of the window. No, he looked the type who liked peace and quiet, but there was something strange about the way he smiled in the photos. His teeth were dead white and he showed them as if he was advertising what he did. Maybe he was. Sylvia said he was a workaholic and a control freak.

But it did bother me that I was having an affair with a married woman, because the only other married woman I ever got involved with was very unhappy in her marriage, and I like to think that I gave her some pleasure she wasn't getting from anywhere else, but she went a bit nuts in the end and ended up going for her husband with a kitchen knife. He was a cruel bastard, like. Treated her like a slave, and he talked to her like she was stupid and humiliated her all the time. When she snapped and went for him with the knife, she could've killed him. When that guy found out about me, he came looking for me. Unlike Alasdair, this guy wasn't a fancy dentist with a big white smile. He was a professional criminal. He ran a massage parlour and he was into all kinds of wheeling and dealing, drugs, the sex trade, stolen goods, you name it. I was in my local with a couple of mates when he came in with a few of his associates. I knew it was him, like, because like Alasdair I'd seen his photo. Not a particularly tall or well-built guy, but you could tell he was a hard nut all the same by the set of his mouth and the way he stood, sticking his mug towards the camera as if it better get him right. And when I saw him moving about the bar, I thought, this guy's dangerous, a coiled spring waiting to go off. An ugly situation developed between his mates and mine. They were making a lot of noise, deliberately like, and a couple of my mates told them to can it, because we were trying to watch a bout on the telly. I'd already finished with her by then, but this guy didn't give a shit about that. So an ugly situation developed and in the end there was a bit of a punch-up.

I tried to stop it happening, like. I'm not in favour of violence outside of the ring. I just did enough to stop these guys beating up my mates, then I went outside with them on my own and I let him break my nose while his pals held me against the wall and that was that. I mean it wasn't as if it hadn't been broken before, and it was a way of bringing the whole situation to an end. So since that happened I've been wary of getting involved with a married woman. Plus, I've never been married myself – it just never happened, don't ask me why – but if I was I wouldn't want somebody else poking my wife. I might be stupid, but I know that even if Sylvia needed a bit of extra on the side – and that woman really did, I'll tell you – that didn't make what we were doing right.

One Friday – and by this time we were actually having a cup of coffee first – I asked her: 'What if he comes home early one day and finds us?'

'He won't, but if he did, you get out the back door sharpish and pretend you're looking at the patio.'

'The patio?'

'Part of it needs to be re-laid. The guy who did it was a cowboy, and now some of it's uneven, and a couple of the slabs have cracked. I keep meaning to get it seen to.'

'Then what happens? I've never laid a patio in my puff. I wouldn't know how to.'

'So? You just look at it, tell me you'll send an estimate, then you disappear and I get someone else to fix it.'

'You've got it all worked out, eh?'

She just shrugged. 'Even if he found out, he wouldn't do much. He'd just make me promise to break it off.'

It sounded like she was talking from experience.

'And would you?'

She just shrugged again. Then the rope comes out of the bag and it's time for Pongo here to get his exercise.

Alasdair never did come home early, never caught us in the act. As far as I know he's still none the wiser, unless she decided to tell him, like, and I can't see why she would do that. They're probably just ticking along as usual. I wouldn't be surprised if she's already found a replacement for yours truly, somebody who's into the really kinky stuff. That's what put me off, in the end. The stuff with the rope was one thing, just a bit of playing around, but she started to get other ideas. She wanted me to do things I didn't really want to do. Coming in the back door, I didn't like that one bit, then all kinds of other stuff – sex toys, bondage suits. Maybe that's what Alasdair and her were into, but it makes me feel dirty just thinking about it even now. When she started to wear the rubber stuff and wanted me to slap her around a bit, then brought out a kind of leather lash with tongues, I thought: enough's enough. Soon after that I told her I wanted to finish it. I told her what was bothering me was sleeping with a married woman. I don't think she really believed me, but she took it in her stride. I suppose she knew it had to end some time. To be honest I think the real reason I got out was because something about it had started to smell bad to me, like in the ring when you start to feel things going against you and you know you're going to lose, so I threw in the towel before things got worse.

I stopped going to the gym on Fridays after that, then I changed to another gym. Then I don't know what happened, I started to get bored with it. Eyeing up all those young things doing their workouts on the machines, and me old enough to be their dad, probably older than their dads. I decided to give the gym a miss for a while, and I haven't been back since. I still exercise though, still like to keep myself in shape. I still do the isometrics and the running, and I still like to do a bit of rope.

Dawn Wood

School of Body and Blood

The fly that had flitted between our folders
the previous evensong decided to up the ghost
in the communion chalice, the Provost noticed,
when he stood in the Lady Chapel, ready
to down the remaining, consecrated host,
at the retiral of the Bishop. Our Bishop
would have been amused at the hygienic Blood
of Our Lord widening its remit to include
bluebottle and all, now buried in wine
in the church back-yard, except that he's just
a white-haired boy, and, as his wife adjusts
his vast cassock, his eyes are asking from a face
of chalk dust, about the writing on the blackboard –
Have I done enough? Isn't this enough?

Roslyn

for Yvonne

William moseys past scaffolding, knows nothing
of turnstiles or Dan Brown and slinks to his pew
for pats from pilgrims. Restoration is ruining
the dank acoustic but *poverty of the heart is a good thing*,
a hymn from Taizé rises with singers in the vault –
those who are not fumbling for the page
in one of the two battered copies of text.
I honestly thought, in the café in Ikea after we left,
when you said *Oh what fun! we sang so much about light…*
and started rummaging in your handbag,
that you'd secreted one set, and, if I'd pocketed
the second, wouldn't that have put a stop
to the Taizé group and their crusade in catacombs,
catalysts for happiness, purring from cradle to crypt?

Trinity Sunday

God the Mother, God the Daughter –
that leaves she, radiant and blowy
who toppled my white lilac on Trinity Sunday,
the one after Pentecost, leaving every floret
of every flower on the lawn, unfading
for the low sun to set, each one vying,
all that is, is our shape, as if the sky
was riven to anchor living stars, fallen
and the trunk made a seat for me
where she laid her hand over mine
in that game of stacking hands,
to play with minds, the laughter of mind
over mind, many hands making light
in the chancel apex of her arbour.

Daniel Jewesbury

Belfast – Our Time, Our Place

What a year. During 2012, while economic forecasts were being repeatedly revised downwards, and more and greater cuts to general public provision were enthusiastically promised by the coalition government, the UK gambled everything on a Keynesianism of the spectacle: billions were lavished on the Olympics and Paralympics, and the countless sideshows that accompanied them nationwide as part of the London 2012 Festival. The phrase 'bread and circuses' hardly does justice to misallocation of public funds on such a scale. Whether the games cost £9bn, or £11bn, or some other figure that hasn't yet been calculated, we are breathlessly assured that it was worth it because of the returns that are going to accrue in the months and years to come (returns which are unfortunately, by their very nature, so often unquantifiable in mere numerical terms). What has been promised is a kind of heritage of the future, a Govian-Schamaesque heroic history that is still to be made: tomorrow belongs to us.

Meanwhile, however, the UK is a nation increasingly ill at ease with itself. Our government explains that continued recession is caused not by the disappearance of demand in the economy but by instability in Europe; there is therefore no need to revise the coalition's economic strategy, even if they can't agree amongst themselves exactly what it is. Simultaneously, public attitudes are turning against the poor, those on benefits, and even the disabled (could it be that the Paralympics had the unintended effect of making 'disability' appear to be simply a refusal to get off your arse and stop whinging?) The fourth estate seems genuinely confused, waiting anxiously for Lord Leveson's report while fulminating against foreign scoundrels for printing pictures of a nearly-naked duchess that they would love to have scooped themselves. The constitutional position of the UK is more uncertain than it has been for many decades: the national government is composed of parties that are in opposition or have no representation at all in the devolved assemblies, each of which has different powers to all the others, and different parties standing in it; and a referendum on Scottish independence is now set to take place in 2014.

Yet none of the regions can be more anomalous than Northern Ireland, the only one of the four 'nations' of the UK not to be a nation at all. Even in deciding what to call it one exposes one's political bias (throughout this text I've used the names 'Northern Ireland' and 'the North' interchangeably, mainly because I have a reasonably complex and ambivalent set of understandings about its political and economic viability and legitimacy). Northern Ireland is effectively doubly disenfranchised from UK politics. The only one of the parties theoretically capable of forming a UK government to stand in Northern Irish elections is the Conservatives; in 2005, they stood in only three of the North's eighteen seats and lost their deposits in each one. In 2010 they merged with the Ulster Unionists to form the 'Ulster Conservatives and Unionists – New Force', which resulted in the UUP losing their only Westminster seat. With no access to a significant democratic mandate at Westminster, we also have an Assembly in which sectarianism is actually written into its procedures: the terms of the power-sharing mechanism, used to ensure cross-community support for legislative motions passed at Stormont, mean that each member must declare themselves as Unionist or Nationalist on taking their seat. And the list of powers reserved by Westminster, which of course is different to those reserved in Scotland or Wales, means that the Assembly is mostly just a glorified parish council, unable to raise its own revenues or to set its own total expenditure. It is desperately lacking in political expertise, infested with sectarian clientelism, and boasts several members – including ministers – who refuse to accept the scientific basis of evolution.

On a bright, blowy morning in April, I walked from my home in north Belfast to an arts centre on the Shankill Road. At the invitation of a friend, I was attending the launch of the 'Greater Shankill Neighbourhood Renewal Area Action Plan'. Community activists had talked and bargained and consulted for two years to produce the document, which is a familiar mix of bullet points, numbered paragraphs, statistics, and tables of aspirational 'action points' – the technocratic language that government has taught civil society to use whenever it wishes to engage it in conversation.

We drank tea and ate croissants with jam as the plan was introduced in the enormous main hall, normally used for gigs or plays. Projected onto the screen were the usual laudable intentions – plans to address the chronic unemployment and the lack of skills among the working-age population, plans to make the Shankill 'an area where drugs are not easily available', and this time, an emphasis on 'wrap-around' support, a piece of jargon which apparently means putting families at the centre of the strategy: the aim of the community is to support the family, as it in turn supports the individual, from the cradle to young adulthood and beyond. The report is only the latest in a pile of similar plans, assessments, feasibility studies and the like, produced by the huge number of community groups and voluntary organisations struggling for recognition in 'post-conflict' Belfast; but even now, fourteen years after the signing of the Good Friday Agreement, it's still all about accessing the most basic of necessities.

The University of Ulster is planning a major new development at its Belfast campus, on the doorstep of Lower Shankill, but the Action Plan mentions nothing about young people from the area aspiring to study there. It says nothing about 'learning' being an aspiration in its own right; although the plan is seen as an approach for the next twenty years, there seems to be no expectation that kids in the Shankill should or could go to university (whatever the merits of university education may or may not now be). The idea is just too far off, the suggestion being that the people of the Shankill know their place, haven't started getting notions about themselves. The Action Plan is a piece of organised pleading for there to be some way of keeping this extremely poor community alive, but the launch was notable for the absence of any well-placed political representatives. The two councillors who attended (from the DUP and SDLP) made no contribution. Across the peaceline, in the Falls Road, the development of an agenda such as this would be driven from the outset by Sinn Féin and the community groups it works with. On the Shankill, community activists have a harder time persuading their elected representatives to show some interest in their cause.

The most obvious and dispiriting thing about the whole event, though, is that the document exists in a kind of economic vacuum, hermetically sealed within its own good intentions. There is no recognition that even the very humble hopes itemised on page after page, in table after table, are all the time getting further and further away from being realised. Northern Ireland has yet to feel the full effect of the public sector cuts. We're less than halfway through a five-year spending round that will see our block grant from London cut by 10 per cent in real terms, with spending on capital projects slashed by nearly 40 per cent; this in a region that raises from its own taxes barely half what it spends. As capital spending disappears, so more of the construction firms that prospered during the boom go bankrupt each week. Schools, libraries and health centres will close. As public transport subsidies decrease, fares will go up, and communities will become more isolated. Funding to the community and voluntary sector, a crucial layer of Northern Ireland's efflorescent bureaucracy, will become minimal (the next generation of 'action plans' will aspire to less, and achieve less again). And some time after the next election, the deferred water charges, for which no political party wanted to take responsibility, despite their arguments about the need for alignment with the rest of the UK, will finally be introduced.

Across town, one item of capital spend was, however, completed on time, at a public cost of around £60m. The Titanic Belfast exhibition centre, in the middle of the dusty brownfield wasteland that used to be the shipyards (now dubbed – what else? – the Titanic Quarter), opened in time to be the star attraction in a festival organised by the Tourist Board and City Council to commemorate the sinking of the ship a century ago. The building is astounding, gravity-defying; its four cantilevered 'wings', resembling towering ships' bows, look a little like a giant arrowhead planted in the ground. Belfast wags who have commented that it looks more like an iceberg than the Titanic have inadvertently divined Texan architect Eric Kuhne's original inspiration for the building, which is in fact meant to encapsulate that dynamic, violent moment when steel struck ice in the frozen north Atlantic. Inside are various 'experiences' descriptive of the making, sailing, sinking and selling of the famous liner, which for £13.50 the visitor can explore. I had an opportunity to look inside during a promenade theatre production put on by Belfast company Kabosh in the opening week. It is predictably impressive, with exciting views both in and outside the building. Surely, as Titanic museums go, it is the biggest and most elaborate in the world. It is true that the building has already had more than 500,000 visitors, and far surpassed its first year projections. The Northern Ireland Audit Office, however, believes that it needs to receive

290,000 paying visitors *every year thereafter* if it is to break even, and predicts that, after the initial flurry of interest, it can expect annual audiences only very slightly above that, around 305,000. Notwithstanding initial interest in this centenary year, the building is running on slender margins.

Whether you view the sad story of the Titanic as primarily a tragic loss of life, a catastrophic failure of individual human judgement, or a clear case of corporate manslaughter, the anniversary festivities in Belfast were peculiarly inappropriate. The chilly first half of April saw light shows in the drizzle, an open-air concert sponsored by MTV outside Titanic Belfast, and a slew of other theatrical productions, film screenings, exhibitions, walking tours and themed banquets (this must surely be the first time in a hundred years that Consommé Olga has appeared on so many menus). The Titanic Festival, however, is only one aspect of a comprehensive, ambitious marketing drive devised by the Northern Ireland Tourist Board, which has seen the whole of 2012 branded with a logo of red, blue and yellow ribbons bearing the slogan 'Our Time, Our Place'. (It seems strange that the Tourist Board should use the possessive plural in this introverted way; writer Colin Graham suggested in Belfast's satirical *Vacuum* newspaper that the recent campaigns try to speak to two audiences at once, constructing an image of 'us', for external consumption, as dynamic, optimistic, youthful, relaxed, jocular, welcoming and confident, while simultaneously reminding 'us' that we have to behave, and play nicely when the guests are here.)

As the summer progressed, we were able to enjoy Northern Ireland's contribution to the Olympics spin-off London 2012 Festival. The high point of this was a 'spectacular' at the end of June called 'Land of Giants', in which the 'icons' and 'legends' of Belfast's past and present – Fionn mac Cumhaill, Lemuel Gulliver (Swift drew inspiration for his story from the topography around Belfast), the Harland & Wolff cranes Samson and Goliath, the Titanic (again) and, of course, us, who are 'giant in ideas, talent and heritage' – converged in a spasm of 'acrobatics, aerial dance, physical performance, music, special effects and pyrotechnics', and drizzle.

There was hardly time to recover from all this pageantry (meagre cost: £1.2m) before the parading that accompanies any Northern Irish summer was underway. This year's marching season was particularly active. On the Twelfth of July, as they waited for the main march to depart, a loyalist band from the Shankill Road decided to create a new 'flashpoint' where none had previously existed, by playing sectarian songs outside a Catholic church in the north city centre. This had the desired effect of provoking statements of outrage from Catholic residents nearby, and a theme was set for the summer. Two major marches in August (the first time the Royal Black Perceptory's 'Last Saturday' march had been held in Belfast) and September (marking the centenary of the signing, by half a million men and women, of the Ulster Covenant against the Third Home Rule Bill) duly returned to this spot, and photographers, camermen, and the professionally offended were ready for them. It seems likely that the loyalists' strategy, inasmuch as they inadvertently stumbled upon one – wilfully igniting and then painstakingly neutralising a new locus of conflict – was to find a new front for their ongoing campaign against the Parades Commission, the body which decides what marches and processions can take place, and under what conditions. The side effect of this political game was that attention was mostly diverted away from what they had hoped would be a story of celebration and commemmoration at the Covenant event – a further attempted recuperation of loyalism as 'heritage' – and focused instead on the possibility of another violent confrontation in the city centre.

All in all, then, the Covenant centenary may have been something of a missed opportunity; this history anyway proves harder to neutralise than the decline and dereliction of the shipyards has been. This mixed story may give us some indication of how the approaching decade of equally uncomfortable centenaries – of the Easter Rising, the slaughter of the Ulster Division in the Battle of the Somme, the Sinn Féin landslide in the 1918 general election, the War of Independence, the Anglo-Irish Treaty and the foundation of Northern Ireland itself in 1921 – might be worked for public (and especially tourist) consumption. The Executive has set itself a goal of earning £1bn a year from all tourism by 2020. If it hopes to achieve this, then it needs some strategy by which not only to neutralise but to capitalise on those recurrent opportunities for the North's historical and political background to erupt once again into the foreground.

For the moment, though, we can draw a little breath as we wait for the next carnival to roll up, with 2013 marking Derry's year as UK City of Culture, and the whole bloody business, as Samuel Beckett put it, starting all over again.

So is this it? Is all this din of celebration and self-congratulation our evidence that the post-conflict promises have finally been realised? In the decade after the Agreement, Belfast reverberated to the noise of construction. It felt like a small eastern European nation emerging from state socialism: areas of the city were zoned and rezoned, deals were struck in private, and vast speculative building projects commenced. Meanwhile, experiments were conducted with privatising the public realm: the new shopping centre at Victoria Square, luxury brands in tow, became an unofficial city centre, and the various public agencies drew plans explaining how 'retail-led regeneration' would provide the means to escape our painful recent history. The streetscape was remodelled with gratuitous public art able to speak to us of our history and our future, while helpfully pointing the way to the next department store. New buildings rose – among them the tallest residential building in Ireland, the Obel tower; and, just occasionally, old ones accidentally burned down, as they tend to do in a rapidly redeveloping city. Homeowners saw house prices record the fastest rises in the whole of the UK (admittedly from a much lower base), with some properties trebling in value in just five years.

Then, in 2008, it ground to a halt. As investors and speculators in the Republic of Ireland saw their loans recalled and their banks bailed out, work stopped on a number of high-profile city centre projects, with others not even commencing. Only in 2011 did the extent of northern developers' exposure to the Republic's crisis finally become clear, as the National Assets Management Agency, the Republic's 'bad bank', published a list of sites in the North that had passed into the reluctant ownership of the taxpayers of the Irish Republic. This was not the way we had expected reunification might take place.

All this is familiar enough, hardly distinctive. What was different about Belfast, and about Northern Ireland as a whole (although the extent of redevelopment has remained extremely uneven across the region) was the particular 'moral economy' that was quite quickly created during the boom, and which persisted through successive interruptions and prorogations of the Assembly, indeed was the single constant throughout. It entails, in essence, a refinement of the argument which maintains that there can be 'no alternative' to speculator-driven redevelopment. In 'normal' societies, this argument is a repetition of the general abandonment of the notion of public good: the final, unarguable victory of trickle-down economics in the urban sphere. In Belfast this took on an added dimension; since there could be no alternative to this model for regeneration, and since our choice could only be between the hope and promise of peace on the one hand, and the tangible threat of continued war on the other, private developers found themselves imbued with a new moral mission. They would be the ones who really delivered the peace, in brick, concrete, glass and steel; the politicians' contribution was merely to learn to behave for long enough to allow it to happen (particularly since planning powers have yet to be devolved to elected local representatives). Very quickly it became apparent that to oppose this prescription for urban redevelopment meant to oppose peace itself. The idea was given form when a property developer, responsible for a range of controversial projects around the city, was appointed as the Chair of the new Policing Board.

While carte blanche – or rather, active encouragement – was thus being given to private speculators, local bureaucrats and politicians were becoming especially interested in the opportunity to compete with European and international cities for a range of potentially valuable cultural prizes. This market had been hot since at least the early 1990s, as contemporary city-states detached themselves from their regions, rebranded themselves into corporate entities and bid to be European Capital of Culture, or to host a biennale or, perhaps, an international sporting championship. Belfast's first stab at this racket was marked by some ignominy, when the bid to be Capital of Culture in 2008 was unsuccessful; but the lesson was learned that the circuits of capital are international, and that our competitors are not in Dublin, Derry or Glasgow, but Barcelona, Melbourne and Dubai.

The political conflict, meanwhile, became sublimated into a cultural contest, about symbols and languages, and even this has started to lose its venom (the summer's events notwithstanding). Both the DUP and Sinn Féin have become adept at facing in two different directions at once: towards their electoral base, and (jointly) towards the market and its demands. The base is still defined in sectarian terms, and the address to them remains clearly about protecting 'our' interests. It might be expected that the requirement on the two main parties to choreograph their joint approach to business would bring with it a necessity to imagine some kind of shared future, but this is impossible while 'power-sharing' is constructed in such nakedly sectarian terms. The two parties are locked in an interdependent embrace, with no interest in articulating a shared, public belonging that can go beyond crudely ethnopolitical 'provision'; so long as they are able to maintain the sectarian balancing act, the job of 'management' can go on indefinitely.

The reflex reaction to such complaints is to mutter that the past can so easily come back if we aren't careful. Yet these days, there is very little stomach for the conflict as it was; increasingly, however, there is an anomic, impotent rage at the continued failure of the devolved administration to provide for the poorest here, who continue to fail educationally, get the worst jobs or no jobs at all, and die younger. The opposite of the management of Northern Ireland for global business interests is not renewed sectarian violence, it's a class anger that crosses ethnoreligious lines – a nightmare that the politicians prefer not to countenance.

It's a commonplace to hear that Northern Ireland's bloated public sector is unsustainable and must now be cut. One third of employment is in the public sector, and another third is directly or indirectly dependent on it. Public expenditure stands at 70 per cent of GDP. But, beyond the familiar argument that the private sector is underdeveloped in the North (so much for the illusory peace dividend), what creates this imbalance is, once again, the sectarianised administration of devolution: from the neighbourhood, and up to the topmost level of the state, we are awash with semi-state and state-funded organisations, all busily publishing regeneration plans and conducting consultations. At the level of the various government agencies, the confusion of responsibilities between local authorities, the Departments of Social Development, Regional Development, and Environment, the different regeneration quangos, and of course the Northern Ireland Office means that it is impossible for ordinary citizens, acting in their own right, to put any effective pressure on policymakers. In turn that interaction between ordinary people, public bodies and politicians has become professionalised, with community groups and partnership boards proliferating in the breach, and any democratic accountability obscured.

Can we really not imagine this place any differently? I went to see a friend, Leontia Flynn, a poet (she's constantly referred to in Northern Ireland as a 'local poet', much to her bemusement – does a local poet have some sort of public function? To what, exactly, are they really local?) She's had her crack at criticising the tawdriness and banality of our post-conflict society. She found it ironic that the arts, which had flourished, in certain ways, during the most difficult times, were now merely a minor element in the rebranding of Belfast, and of Northern Ireland; creativity, or culture in the vaguest, most general sense, are obviously valuable buzzwords in any adman's spiel about the place, but not usually in any engaged or sustained way. Poetry, she admits, continues to be something that is saleable about the North, and she understands that she too is expected, when she travels to readings abroad (she was just back from Poland), to 'represent', somehow, this new Northern Ireland (something else that causes her some bemusement). But even while the tourist brands sell images of who 'we' are, and the next generation of Northerners, like young people everywhere else, happily accept their duty to commodify and consume virtual 'selves', through social networks, designer labels and musical scenes, it doesn't appear that a 'culture' which was often so introspective during the Troubles has much that is genuinely communicable to offer to anyone outside, at least not something that is actually 'about' us; or here. We've stopped talking about ourselves, to some degree, because we're not sure where exactly we are yet. Graham Walker, a professor of politics at Queen's University, told me that his students want to write about the political conflict in the 1970s or '80s, but have very little to say about the committee structure of the Northern Ireland Assembly.

The Greater Shankill Neighbourhood Renewal Area Action Plan contains a section titled 'It Needs A Designation'. The partnership who authored the plan understand that they need their area 'designated' – branded – if they are to stand some chance of success. 'This plan needs a structure and the Greater Shankill needs a designation to realise it... In Belfast we have done this around physical development. It was called "Laganside" and has its latest manifestation in Titanic Quarter or around cultural development as in Cathedral Quarter.' The Shankill is desperate for a brand.

Another friend, a former actor from the North who's now a psychotherapist, talked to me about Northern Ireland in the context of the family therapy she practices. We spoke about the lack of an 'identity' that can create a single, functional, inclusive society in Northern Ireland. The Good Friday Agreement and the peace process swept away a society, such as it was, but made no effort to replace it with something else, indeed the whole point was not to replace with anything else; the history of the last fourteen years has been about the impossibility of arriving at this 'something else' whilst ideas of sovereignty and nationality remain so irreconcilable, so incommensurate.

I talked with Graham Walker about the threat to this fragile sense of collective self from the Scottish referendum on independence. Unionists have reacted with some hysteria to the plans: Sir Reg Empey, former leader of the

UUP, announced that Scottish independence could 'reignite the difficulties we have just managed to overcome', while John Taylor, now Lord Kilclooney, wrote to *The Scotsman* that if parts of Scotland voted to remain in the Union, it would be better to offer partition than to subjugate them to the will of the majority. In a speech at the annual conference of the British-Irish Association in September this year, First Minister Peter Robinson made a detailed case for the continuation of the Union, and even seemed to suggest (in somewhat more historically measured tones than those of Kilclooney) that the partition of Ireland has not been an entirely untrammelled success: 'While Ulster was always a place apart on the island of Ireland, partition changed things – and not just for Northern Protestants, but for Southern Catholics and Southern Protestants for that matter, as well'. Reporting of the speech in the media was limited to Robinson's claim that the call for independence could be defeated 'with a Saltire in one hand and a Union Flag in the other', a strange take on the IRA's stated strategy in the 1980s of achieving independence 'with a ballot box in one hand and an Armalite in the other'.

Nonetheless I wondered whether there mightn't be a pocket of opinion within Unionism that might, if push came to shove, prefer to align itself with an independent Scotland rather than a distant, 'disinterested' England. Walker feels that members of the DUP might harbour a sentimental affection of this kind, but that even they would recognise that it couldn't be done in reality. If the Scots do vote against independence, it will probably mark the end of the Barnett Formula, by which the block grant has been distributed across the UK since the 1970s. Moreover it could mark the beginning of discussions about a more equally devolved, or even fully federalised UK (something else which Robinson's BIA speech accepted needed to be more thoroughly examined). Both these measures could, in the long run, make an enormous difference to the political and economic culture of the North: Barnett, particularly, should be replaced with a formula based on needs, rather than on a simple headcount, especially given the massive changes to the consitutional arrangement since it was implemented. Walker believes that the devolved nations have not made enough of their opportunity to work in partnership from the fringes of the Union, and nor have they used the range of institutions available to them – particularly the British-Irish Council (no relation of the BIA), a body set up under the terms of the Good Friday Agreement as an 'East-West' counterbalance to allay Unionist fears about proposed North-South bodies. Despite existing since 1998, the Council only established a full-time secretariat earlier this year; it has a remit to meet and issue communiqués on a range of topics – including languages, spatial planning, housing and the environment. A mechanism through which the nations can speak to one another bilaterally, without the involvement of London, the Council could offer a degree of collective bargaining power to the Irish, Northern Irish, Scots and Welsh. But the ad hoc, piecemeal way in which devolution was delivered by New Labour means anyway that the status quo is unlikely to be tenable for very long. 'The more anomalies persist between the manner in which devolution has been realised in the different parts of the UK, the more it grates and the looser the fabric becomes,' Walker warns.

As it stands, Belfast at the end of 2012 continues to be a blank slate, upon which can be written the most lurid fantasies of urban planners, undead private developers and tourism wonks. A proposal recently published by one government agency for a scrappy patch of land beside the River Lagan included sketches of a zip-cord stretched between the banks of the river. The worrying lesson of Titanic Belfast is that anything is now possible, if the right people decide that it's necessary. They are, of course, doing it for our benefit.

Will Stone

Fir Forest

Rising up too darkly for men,
they sow confusion in their coldness,
haul their gradient into the ravine.
Always enough space for a hanging
over the off-cuts of scattered huts,
swallowing dust, thickly painting
over the impertinent sound of saws.
Canopies are dense but seem poor,
monotonous sap and needle speech
that draws foreboding in towards you.
Bombed cathedral, gutted house,
abyss of whispers, forbidden barn
of casually blackened wounds.
Stolen bird calls sifted, counted.
A grey procession of faith
that moves on without you,
hoarder of the stream's silver
the cowbell's gold, but forbids
passage through the un-trod cloister,
where only the lonely one passes,
sees sky through rents of branches,
recognises the full moon as the face
that appeared at the window,
unconsciously drawn, like the rest
to the screams of a new birth.

Where the Airmen Are

Find where the airmen are,
in the secret of Brussels cemetery.
Their plot is different, precise, scripted
shorn and buffed like a bowling green
and their headstones, pale and cool
as abbey walls in August are identical,
but for the names...
Another five who died in flames,
A whole Lancaster crew.
The oldest was only twenty-five.
Side by side they lie and cradled
now in the box scented breeze,
in the slowly traversing willows of rain.
Unvisited except for the taciturn mower
and a hardy few placing wreathes
in irritable November weather.
Their mothers of English shires
all rest now too in turf caped tombs
or in dusty urns in the honeycomb
of suburban crematoriums.
But one of them, who stroked his cap
on the coffin, had asked
for words to be engraved here.
 'Our beloved Dennis
He believed in England
and fought to keep her free'
Mother.

Seventeen Days

The epitaph
 'Sleep well little man…'
for barely awake
after seventeen days you died.
Gone before you relished the wing
quiver of your first thrush, or watched
the hawk intimidate into action
those undecided first hours of spring.
Gone after a brief base struggle,
a plunge from the nest when
to no avail you felt the rushing air,
down to where no lost lamb bleat
could reach you,
no damp bracken scent off Exmoor.
Interred before you saw your feet
ghost stir the sand in clear water.
No time to inhale a fistful of soil,
crumbling, almost moist, poised
to give hope and infinite good.
Like this one from the Cornish graveyard
wild primrose bristling with bone roots,
filaments to be planted far from here
with the usual expectation…
'Sleep well little man…'
with your poor catch of hours
littered about you.

Reviews

Mo Said She Was Quirky Hamish Hamilton. ISBN 9780241144565. £14.99
James Kelman

James Kelman is quirky. He once asked 'What actually is the proletariat? Or for that matter the bourgeoisie? How do you recognise a class of folk? Or a race of people?', and answered his own question by saying, 'You recognise them by general characteristics. When we perceive a member of a class we are not perceiving an individual human being, we are perceiving an idea, an abstract entity, a generality; it is a way of looking that by and large is the very opposite of art'. *Mo Said She Was Quirky* is framed by an encounter with 'a pair of homeless guys'. How can you tell 'a pair of homeless guys'? Do you follow them home and make sure they don't arrive at any such domestic destination? In the case of Helen, a London casino dealer from backward Glasgow in a world where life's a gamble, on her way home from work in a cab, 'You could tell just by looking'. Yet Helen's clients at the casino, rich men with homes, acted like they had 'no homes to go to'.

Danny, the taxi driver, a man in the mould of Helen's boorish ex-husband, sees 'Alkies', but Helen sees something familiar, a piece of her past. Her long-lost big brother Brian, her childhood 'horsie', might just be one of the homeless guys in question. He ain't homeless, he's her brother. And if he is her brother, and he is homeless, then it's something she can fix, even if she herself feels rootless and unsettled, especially if she feels that way. She can find her way home by finding a home for him. Still, her certainty that the pair are homeless jars with her statement that the whispering of her fellow passenger 'was prejudice pure and simple'. Is it possible to think, to write, without prejudice, bloodlessly, with absolute political correctness, whatever that might look like? You can never tell just by looking. Helen is annoyed at her friend's comments about this unkempt pair, 'like as if something was wrong with being tall and with a beard, or being thin', when it might just mean you 'were homeless and didnt have any scissors or razors'.

This is a novel about homelessness and about how individuals are haunted by families and communities and cultures that they believe they've left behind. It's also a novel about damaged masculinity, the only type in town, about the damage that men do, and few of the men in Helen's life escape the lash, not even her good guy Asian boyfriend, Mohammed, Mo for short, from 'Middlesex' by name and nature, though both he and her father and Mr Adams, with whom she has a beautifully rendered affair, get lighter strokes, unlike other men. And men are others, foils to Helen's self. Her friend Ann

Marie dubs them 'the great lost cause', good for nothing 'except hanging a hat'. Helen's reflections on 'the male animal' are among the most moving and telling observations Kelman's characters have produced.

If Mo is one short form of a name that fits the bill, then 'Hel', short for Helen, would be an apt characterisation of her existential crisis. Other people are hell for Helen, but they are also home, Heimlich and unheimlich at one and the same time. Family photographs tell of a daddy's girl, a mammy's boy, and two siblings caught up in a strange, strained relationship, their relationship constructed through the eyes of her parents. People are individuals, families are ghostly apparitions: 'Families were ghosts coming back to haunt you', and 'life is full of shivers'. Thinking of her dead grandparents, Helen reflects that 'Life goes on but people dont, individuals.' Individuals are ghosts by definition, characters conjured up by communities and languages and 'authors', themselves phantasmagorical beings. In *The Ego and Its Own* (1844), Max Stirner argued that the head of 'Man' was full of ghosts. Stirner's real name was Johann Caspar Schmidt, so he had a friendly ghost at the heart of him. It would be tempting at this point to say that families and communities are real, and that the true spectre is the individual, and that Helen is like Nicole Kidman in *The Others* or Bruce Willis in *The Sixth Sense*, the zombie self of possessive and possessed individualism. Tempting, but too late, because Kelman has got there before us, and his interrogation of what it means 'to be', to exist, is as sophisticated as any philosopher's.

Helen is superstitious, imagining her mother's photo landing face down at random and what that might mean. Sophie, Helen's six-year-old daughter, has a strong sense of personhood and her relationship with her mother and with Mo is as toughly tender as Helen's and Mo's relationship, underpinned by hardship. Mo is many things, from one moment to the next, like Helen. He's 'Mr Know-Better', 'Mr Hungry', who 'wouldn't hurt a fly', but he's also 'one good thing that had happened to her, amongst many others'.

Sometimes the reader feels Kelman should get out more, especially when he's in Helen's head and she reflects that 'She didnt like being in taxis with poor people seeing her, as though she was rich, she wasnt'. This seems oddly out of touch, because poor people take taxis all the time, sometimes because living in peripheral housing estates it's cheaper to share a taxi than rely on public transport, especially if you work or party late.

Some of Helen's thoughts read like Kelman's arguments with himself, as a writer who likes to get into the heads of characters, going deep cover while avoiding the risk of ventriloquising and speechifying, of betrayal, that this entails: 'But if everybody was different their thoughts too would be different and all their points of view, everything. You couldnt have everyone different but their thoughts all the same. That was just stupid. Why did people want everybody to be the same? Or act like they did. Usually it was men. But not all the time'. The cult of the individual, whether anarcho-individualism or bourgeois individualism, is a cult of the same. Kelman's art has always struggled with the individualism he inherited from writers like Beckett, middle class eavesdroppers on the poor. Beckett famously said of *Not I*, 'I knew that woman in Ireland… I knew who she was – not "she" specifically, one single woman, but there are so many of those old crones, stumbling down the lanes, in the ditches, beside the hedgerows. Ireland is full of them. And I heard "her" saying what I wrote in *Not I*. I actually heard it'. There is no ventriloquising, no vicariousness, no vagrant tourism in Kelman. The Beckett who could say 'I as a prod of prejudices prefer […] real and radiant individuals to […] our national scene' may sound like Kelman, but Kelman is much more political, and not so much more profound as deeper in a different way. As well as a regretful self, Beckett showed a resentful self. He wrote: 'The mortal microcosm cannot forgive the relative immortality of the macrocosm. The whiskey bears a grudge against the decanter'. The self is the whisky in the jar, the spirit that resents the vessel that contains it. But as Kelman's Helen says, 'People arent whisky'.

Granted, Helen can ask, 'What was Scottishness? She didnt know what it was and it didnt matter because it wasnt her', but she's full of contradictions, and that's what makes her such an incredible creation, such a compelling character, as finely drawn as any of Kelman's protagonists. And she's right too, because the fundamental faultlines that concern her most are around family and gender, and really around gender, because family becomes a way of examining what it means to be a woman, a wife, a mother, a daughter, a girl, a girlfriend.

In *Mo Said She Was Quirky* Kelman is at his brilliant best, but then his consistency and his integrity of purpose, his commitment to his art, are never in doubt. It's pointless to talk about development with Kelman's writing. He's been at the top of his game for thirty years and there's no sign of him flagging, nor is there any sign that the issues that have always driven him, bone-bred issues of justice and language and representation and rights, have been relegated by new political realities. Mo matters, yes, but he's just a mo in Helen's lifetime, her shadow life: 'Shadows of our lives. A shadow of our life. What our lives are. Those shadows, into those shadows'. This is Helen's story, a day in her life that crams all her life into a day, and with it all her shadows and ghosts. Sometimes Alasdair Gray's *Lanark* is seen as doing for Glasgow what Joyce did for Dublin, with Kelman more often compared to Beckett – and there is a very Beckettian ending to this novel – but what Kelman does here with consciousness and narrative is a special achievement, as rich as Molly's monologue. How Helen talks about Mr Adams is an astonishing passage of writing, one of the most subtle renderings of the complexity of desire you'll come across.

Helen asks hard questions. What is a father, a brother, a sister, a mother? What is a family? And she makes the reader, or made this reader, think about what the answers to those questions might be. What Helen is searching for goes to the heart of what it means to be human, the male animal and the female animal. It would be glib to say that Kelman handles the knots of class and gender and race and religion with consummate ease, but that makes those forms of difference sound like the four horsemen of the apocalypse, whereas Kelman's highly individual and human way of approaching cultural difference and identity is much more sophisticated than the current language of criticism would allow. I can imagine teaching this novel. I can also happily conceive of not teaching it, and putting it alongside those cherished books on my shelf that are not there to be the subject of seminars and smart talk, but are there to teach me.

Willy Maley

Bevel. Carcanet. ISBN 9781847771926. £9.95
William Letford

The spoken poem is surrounded by what? Listening, maybe, silence perhaps, other voices, air. These are the interfaces where meaning is made. The poem in a book is surrounded by an equivalent field of white paper – equivalent opportunities for collaboration with the reader – but it's not every poet that chooses to probe that territory: to test its resistances, its rhythmic, interpersonal and contextual implications; to ask how many things it can be likened to. Spatial awareness, whether it measures the small room in Italy, with its empty chairs, and window crammed with mountains, or the ninety-three million miles that comprise an astronomical unit, is clearly a heightened sense for William Letford.

Carcanet have added three-quarter inches of width to Letford's first collection, *Bevel.* (I thought it was worth getting the ruler out because its dimensions so affect the book's impact. Closed, it exceeds my palm; open, it makes a splash in the hands.) The increased page-width corresponds to Letford's gaze on the world: first, it's a provocation – *look, see if a voice comes to haunt this white space* – and second, providing a stage for this wide-eyed, open-minded psyche, which is exemplified in the three-line, three-page '[coffee shop window]': 'only children brave enough/to return my stare' in which the widened format augments the meaning. Each page is a grand sheet of float glass framing a phrase, which gives the reader time to experience the myriad, calculating adjustments we make in a single human encounter. The book was good company: I consumed it in an hour, voraciously; and was delighted that second and third readings continued to reward deeper attention.

Letford works as a roofer. I expect journalists to make much of his profession over the next few years, if he gets the attention he deserves… his working life is a genuine influence on the perspective and impetus of his poems. For a start, he definitely observes from a vantage point. From this metaphorical and actual roof, the universe is realmic and elemental, peopled by pre-Christian deities of sun and fire, come to walk among us as tradesmen and labourers. In 'They speak of the gods', the sky is heaven, and his workmate an opulent, jovial Zeus, moving over the tiles. And when, in '[T-Shirt wrapped around my head]' Letford refuses to equate manual labour with slavery, the sun inflates his shadow to that of a Pharaoh. In these typically reverberating, atavistic moments, Letford is able to communicate huge distances in space and time more effectively than when he employs the imagery of science 'A bassline/Courses like a neutron star counting the immeasurable'.

There are further instances of blurred focus due to over-explication. 'Becoming' – 'It's a powerful sensation. This mixture of pride and sadness' – or ('Helsinki, Finland') – 'cause when you're away even the mundane is novel'. These are a bit of a come-down in a collection demonstrating so much precision and fluency in the unspoken, especially when what Letford calls 'mundane' are usually clear-eyed, humane and honest encounters in gendered, sexual, domestic, familial, historical and astronomical space.

The riddle 'Wit is it', at the opposite extreme, demonstrates Letford's instinct for the unsaid. In this poem, the narrator approaches workmates – as if a council of Jedi knights! – with an unknown question. Their gnomic responses constellate an answer that is both transparent and elusive: 'it's aboot strength, son/Wit kin ye caerry, wit kin yi leave behind'... 'listen tae that, he sade, this is it, a think this is it.' What the question might be is – in the tradition of grail-seeking – for the reader to decide, in collaboration with the poet: the passing of a poem 'from chest to chest' (Letford's manifesto, 'a poem'). And where does this negotiation take place? Reader and writer meet at the perimeters of the text, on the white plain of the page.

In some poems, the white spaces are rhythmic and relative, a kind of musical scoring. In '[it rains]', for example, the rhythm of the turning page marks the passing of time, and the reader is invited to meditate on two sounds: the rain, and the crickets. In 'sex poem number 1' it's sex itself, the experience of articulation ceding to rhythm and sensation.

In others, it's a drawing: the visual representation of some content of the poem. In '[Tshirt wrapped around my head]' it's the cavities in an ancient wall, where time past, present and future (the historic builder, the scorpion and a clutch of eggs) are brought together. In 'Worker' it's apparently the corner of a building, a perfect right-angle. In 'Moths', a rhythmic dazzle of pests sequined over the page and recalling Edwin Morgan's 'French Persian Cats Having A Ball', it represents the scene of domestic devastation.

Finally, the page sometimes becomes the threshold of infinity and possibility. In 'Thurs hunnurs a burds oan the roofs' (a favourite), it's a return to that theme of infinitely-perpetuated potential: 'we're no dodos we kin fly forget aboot the fields Frank look it the sky'. The absence of a final full-stop in this and other pieces recalls the roofless church ('In the mountains of northern Italy') which locals prefer to the 'coffin lid' of the Sistine Chapel. The lid has been blown off these poems.

I (sometimes) agree with Don Paterson (that 'poetry is not a calling, but a diagnosis'[1] – *Bevel*, however, represents an unusually 'healthy' poetry: a triumph of communication rather than the last shot at it. That steady gaze is unusual, in that it invites a genuinely-shared act of linguistic and paralinguistic communion. Reading and rereading *Bevel* is a pre-lapsarian pleasure. It all boils down to widening the eyes, and saying what you see.

Jen Hadfield

Notes
1. http://www.heraldscotland.com/books-poetry/comment-debate/a-post-creative-scotland.2012091643

William Letford's *Bevel* is now available in wide-screen from Carcanet (£9.95).

The Magicians of Edinburgh Polygon. ISBN 9781846972362. £9.99
Ron Butlin

These are Edinburgh poems in the fullest sense. Ron Butlin inhabits Edinburgh in the physical sense, and he has made his city the stage for a dazzling series of riffs on its shape, its size, its gradients, its past, its present, its groans (the traffic, the trams, the weather) and its celebrations. Most of all, its people.

> Magic happens daily on the Bridges, on George Street,
> in Tollcross, a nod from a stranger,
> a quick drink with a friend I've bumped into
> (I never leave home, but meet someone I know.)

And this is the truth: the sight of poet and dog is a common one in EH9 but the poems here are an Edinburgh transformed through his eyes and ears. The Meadows under snow – snowmen multiplying ('The first snowman in the Meadows must have texted his friends') and the light changing ('Let's live for these light-filled days, / this snow-tumbled darkness'). The city's skyscape and the physical reality of its streets are everywhere. The past is a steady background, inescapably, over and over in the poems, something to be lived with:

> That's the past for you – so much background clamour
> to our pavement-table beer

and it changes places constantly in these poems with an all-too-recognisable present, the streets, the people, the tourists, and (a recurrent theme) the city's craze for planning. The trams, ruefully, get a drubbing:

> You plan another plan for the centre of the town,
> You rip the new line out and you start it all again
> & that's what it's all about!

but the hokey-cokey verse is deliberate, for the prevailing language in these poems is affectionate and humorous (in both English and accomplished Scots) rather than abrasive. Butlin's very knowledgeable references to music and composers are another feature: Stockhausen, Schoenberg and Cage are real presences, as is David Hume, in the most successful poem of the collection imagining him settling himself down for the last time. 'Not bothering to set his alarm clock, David Hume took to his deathbed' preparing himself for transition to the Great Unknown despite interruptions, visitors ('Bloody visitors. Hume could hear them barging in through his front door'), discussing him in whispers, their concern for his immortal soul – but in the poem he makes the last journey as a walk to the summit of Arthur's Seat and simply walks on past the summit

> He takes his first step into utter and perpetual darkness
> And the darkness holds
>
> Another step. And then another.
>
> Soon he's walking directly above the city. Unnamed stars and
> undiscovered galaxies congregate around him.
> He knows each step could be his last. *As in life,*
> he whispers, *so let it be in death.*
>
> And smiling to himself alone, he puts his best foot forward.

It sums up the virtues of this collection, the wit, the minimal but effective language, the interplay between past and present totally typical of Butlin's Edinburgh, the transforming of the commonplace through the poet's eye. The book reads well from start to finish, the illustrations and the poet's own brief introductions really adding very little. The value lies in the constantly-shifting and constantly-deft perception of the normal into something abnormal, the traffic jam on the City Bypass, the sudden silences which make the city listen to itself, 'The restless sky, the hesitant sun' reshaping the familiar. A consistently successful collection.

Ian Campbell

Tales from the Mall. Cargo Publishing. ISBN 9781908885012. £9.99
Ewan Morrison

In his 1995 book *Non-Places*, the French anthropologist Marc Augé remarks that 'a space which cannot be defined as relational, or historical, or concerned with identity will be a non-place'. Passing one another as solitary, atomised individuals, visitors to non-places navigate environments from which every trace of the historical past has been excluded, and in which their own identities are recast in generic terms: as driver, customer, traveller, guest. Such spaces – motorways, supermarkets, airports, hotels – exemplify our modernity (or, as Augé would have it, our 'supermodernity'), and none more so than the shopping mall.

In taking these overlit, anonymous, hermetically-sealed structures as the subjects and settings of a book consisting, in substantial part, of pieces of short fiction, Ewan Morrison faces a dilemma: how to summon up emotion, pathos, or epiphany in spaces apparently designed to tranquilise any such intensely cathected expressions of personal history and experience? As one of a pair of 'newly separateds' reflects in the book's first story, malls are favoured locations for absent parents to have access time with their children because they are 'neutral space[s] without prior emotional associations'. As it turns out, however, the very blankness and sterility of the mall serves time and again, in Morrison's stories, to induce a kind of *horror vacui*, as spasms of rage, panic, and despair proliferate across the gleaming concourses and temperature-controlled atria.

Here, a child is lost somewhere in the polished no-man's land between Burger King and Build-a-Bear; a businessman searches for the site of his childhood trauma beneath the tarmac expanse of a mall car park; a Tesco's cashier resorts to shoplifting to suppress her 'déjàs' – a disturbing ability to foresee the future, brought on by the monotony of the checkout; an advertising executive collapses in Habitat, overwhelmed by the array of household products and the fulfilment they seem to promise; a market researcher contemplates suicide when she realises that her life is reducible to the demographic type targeted by a new shopping mall; and a woman's horror at the domestic ubiquity of self-assembly, wood-effect furniture generates a profound phobia of IKEA.

In these short fictions, Morrison succeeds in locating humour, poignancy, and desperation in the homogeneous mall-land that sprawls across and around his home city of Glasgow, a landscape which could (and this, of course, is his point) be anywhere. Perhaps the most substantial and affecting story – the penultimate fictional piece, entitled 'Borders' – begins in the iconic year of 1989 and offers a time-lapse portrait of two decades in the life of a young man as he drifts into and out of radical politics and goes on to accumulate and discard jobs, lovers, cars, hobbies, credit cards, tattoos, recipes, and prescriptions before finally meeting his grimly ironic fate in – where else? – the storeroom of a shopping mall. The story powerfully captures the jitteriness, incoherence, and ambivalence of contemporary life – itself, Morrison implies, nothing more than a vast repository of disposable consumer options.

Morrison's stories amount to a compelling and desolate vision, but they form only one of three strands of his book. Interspersed between these fictional snapshots are anecdotes recounted by those who work and shop in malls in Scotland and the United States and instalments in a history of shopping centres, from the Athenian Agora to Westfield. This combination of genres invites comparison with the idiosyncratic writings of W.G. Sebald, Iain Sinclair, and Douglas Coupland (the latter two, indeed, enthusiastically praise Morrison's book). Maintaining a distinction between modes that Sebald and Sinclair, in particular, renounce in their frequently unclassifiable blends of fiction, essay, memoir, and travelogue, Morrison's work, however, proves to be less innovative in formal and stylistic terms than such resemblances might initially suggest.

One area in which *Tales from the Mall* does assume a distinctly radical edge, however, is in its provocative but persuasive identification of peculiar incidents in the lives of malls as forms of 'urban folklore' akin to the traditional songs and stories preserved by archivists like those in the School of Scottish Studies at the University of Edinburgh. Morrison is quite aware of how distasteful some will find this alignment of contemporary mall culture with deep-rooted folk cultures, but if, as he contends, the 'mallification' of Scotland is 'an historic event, as important as the Jacobite Rebellion and the Highland Clearances', then he is right to insist that even 'in the heart of the anonymous international shopping mall' there are 'indigenous stories worth protecting and celebrating'. The tales Morrison relays again present the processes of 'mallification' as exacting a heavy psychic toll, with anger, violence, suicide, and revenge looming large, albeit disfigured, in the telling, into grotesquely comic forms. As these outlandish episodes accumulate, they come to feel, as Morrison intends, like small but revealing contributions to something like an alternative history of the present.

The third element of Morrison's book, devoted to an account of the changing forms and functions of shopping malls, succeeds on two fronts. Firstly, it stands as a substantial piece of historical and sociological research, densely packed with references to scholarly studies of consumer behaviour and burnished with resonant references to celebrated theorists like Walter Benjamin, Jacques Lacan, Herbert Marcuse, and Fredric Jameson. Secondly, and more subtly, these sections' own impassive, scholarly tone permits them to forego the heavy-handed tactics of polemic and simply present, straightforwardly and without evaluative comment, the hair-raising details of how those running malls leverage planning permission, force competitors out of business, exclude 'undesirable' members of the public, and manipulate customers into buying more than they want or require. Morrison's principled anger is, paradoxically, all the more palpable for remaining implicit behind this deadpan prose with its air of authority and objectivity.

Just occasionally, however, an unmistakeably angry, critical, and oppositional voice breaks through, as when Morrison asks a 'dormant' question whose terms run so starkly contrary to all that is commonsensical and taken for granted under the present dispensation as to appear almost meaningless: 'why do we have so many malls, or for that matter, any malls, at all?' If we do have a need for the mall, Morrison suggests in this timely and powerful book, it is a need manufactured by nothing other than the mall itself.

Paul Crosthwaite

Jade Ladder: Contemporary Chinese Poetry. Bloodaxe Books. ISBN 9781852248956.
£12.00
W.N. Herbert and Yang Lian (eds) with Brian Holton and Qin Xiaoyu

In 1972 the New Writers' Press in Dublin published Michael Harnett's English translation of the *Tao te Ching* by Lao Tzu. Writing about the circumstances of the publication, Trevor Joyce claimed that the Press had negotiated with Hartnett for permission to bring out his version of the *Tao* and Hartnett only agreed on condition that he received a pint of stout for each of the eighty-odd sections of the work. This form of braggadocio ghosts the translation of Chinese writing into Western languages. Chinese is seen as so wholly other that it makes the very notion of translation appear, at best, a clumsy approximation and, at worst, a florid deceit. The ideographic basis of Classical Chinese which was not susceptible to phonological evolution, the clotted density of the language, the grammatical versatility with shifting word classes, the economic use of tense and number and the presence of tonality, were all factors that contributed to the construction of a great wall of impenetrability. The only breaches possible were through the fastidious scholarship of an Arthur Waley or the brash recklessness of an Ezra Pound. In a valuable preface to the anthology under review, W.N. Herbert points out that the missing voices in the endless wrangles about the appropriate way to translate Chinese poetry were the voices of the Chinese poets themselves. For this reason, he is insistent on the act of translation being an act of dialogue, between translator, author and reader. Part of this dialogue involves taking form seriously rather than discarding it as so much empty husk that obscures the bright promise of image. Taking form seriously means, however, extensive reworking of the target language as a 'literal translation from Chinese can read a little as though it might purposively be challenging idiomatic convention, whatever its original intent' (p.25). Poorly digested grammar produces the easy upset of the postmodern. In this context, the relative openness of British poetry to earlier poetic traditions rather than the schismatic fanfare of making the new perpetually new, allows for a translation practice that captures the contemporary Chinese poetic conversation between modernity and classical antecedents.

The anthology, which includes around 200 poems by over 60 poets, is divided into two parts. The first part and the most substantial in terms of the numbers of poets included covers what are called 'Lyric Poems'. The second part is divided into five sections and covers 'neo-classical poems', 'sequences', 'experimental poems' and 'long poems'. Each of the sections has a brief introduction by the writer and critic, Qin Xiaoyu. All of the poets presented in the anthology have grown up in Communist China and a number have direct experience of traumatic events such as the Cultural Revolution and the brutal repression following the Tiananmen Square massacre. Many of the poems which feature under the heading of 'Lyric Poems' are strewn with images of menace and brokenness and loss alongside the more familiar vocabulary of kinship ties and restorative nature. Bei Dao who opens the anthology speaks of 'The Art of Poetry':

> in the great house to which I belong
> only a table remains, surrounded
> by boundless marshland
> the moon shines on me from different corners
> the skeleton's fragile dream still stands in the distance, like an
>   undismantled scaffold
> and there are muddy footprints on the blank paper
> the fox which has been fed for many years
> with a flick of his fiery brush flatters and wounds me

Sitting at a solitary table in the great house of Chinese language and culture, the skeletons and scaffolds are unmistakeable features of the poetic landscape. Zhong Ming places a line by the 9th century poet Han Shan as an epigraph to 'Eating with Lamas, Zhao Jue Temple, Chengdu': 'All I smell is humans becoming ghosts'.

In the poetry of Duo Duo, Yan Li, Yang Lian, Zhai Yongming, Gu Cheng, Liao Yiwu, Zhou Lunyou, Song Lin, Chen Dongdong, Hu Dong, Zhang Zao and Song Wei, the ghosts are there and they mingle, ghosts that emerge from a past that is irretrievably past yet tantalisingly close and ghosts that fill the present with the betrayed promises of hope and liberation:

> my soul has had the shit beaten out of it
> in this instant the world is a great ship
> and we are locked up in the hold
> glued to the wall and intently listening to the boundless waters
> and the other even vaster waters of nothingness
> like an arrow piercing the heart
>   (Liao Yiwu 'New Year's Eve in Jail')

Poets like Song Wei, Yi Sha and Hu Xudong corral satire and a carefully measured derision to lay bare the often cruel mixture of the absurd and the purposeful that fills their days in the New China. Much of the poetry in the first part of the anthology has a dense (though not hermetic) allusiveness so that the reader is constantly left guessing as to the wider resonance of specific images and tropes. This is no fault of the translation but an integral part of a poetic idiom that suggests rather than proclaims. Bai Hua in 'Autumn's Weapons' gives voice to his own form of bewilderment:

> at this time, in Chengdu
> everybody's in my face
> giving me cars
> giving me extremes
> giving me violence and the market

Hua is something of an exception, however, in his anguished directness and the dramatic changes in Chinese life over the last two decades in many of the poems are secreted away in random comments and charged images.

One of the highlights of the anthology is the inclusion of 'Narrative Poems' by Sun Wenbo, Zhang Zao, Zhu Zhu and Sun Lei. These are more extended developments of a particular idea or conceit and the poems are compelling examples of condensed poetic moves which both intrigue and illuminate. Zhang Zao's 'Death Sentence on the German Soldier Shermanski' ends on a note of candid bafflement:

> Hey, shoot me in a vital organ.
> Don't shoot me in the heart.
> Katya, my darling…
> I have died a death – really, what is death?
> Death is just like how the others died.

What is notable is that the poems and poets featured in the 'Sequences' and 'Long Poems' have a similar kind of inspired momentum and it is gratifying that the second part of the anthology allows the non-Chinese reader to move beyond the short lyric which has been so dominant in Western perceptions of Chinese Poetry. In a concluding essay to the *Jade Ladder* anthology, 'Phrases That Shall Be Musical in the Mouth', Brian Holton claims that 'our job in this book is to show the English reader contemporary Chinese poetry, and to use every means at our disposal to show as much of it as possible, warts and all, complexity and all, glory and all' (p.350). In this the editors and translators of the anthology have been signally successful. In particular, the stated concern for the musicality and an attentiveness to rhythmic coherence in the translated poems rewards the reader with much that is to be valued. On a recent visit to China, Goran Malmqvist, a sinologist and one of the eighteen members of the Swedish Academy who awarded this year's Nobel Prize for Literature to the novelist Mo Yan claimed, 'Many Chinese poets are qualified enough to be given the Nobel Prize in Literature... but it all depends on the translation.' If the Academy is looking for a vade-mecum for any future Nobel Prizes to be awarded to Chinese poets, they need look no further.

Michael Cronin

NW. Hamish Hamilton. ISBN: 9780241144145. £18-99
Zadie Smith

Sometimes when reading a writer you get the sense that they may have reached the end of a certain way of writing or, at the very least, the end of a way of writing about a certain kind of subject. Such is the impression I get from reading *NW,* Zadie Smith's fourth novel. This might, I suppose, appear a curious sentiment when we consider that Smith returns in *NW* to one of her most persisting preoccupations: the emotional, cultural and racial geographies of that small patch of North-West London ('Oh how I miss the folks back home in Willesden Green', in the words of one of her novel's disembodied narrators) that she has made so spectacularly her own. But *NW* is, for all its rhythmic subtleties and suppleness, linguistic energy and inventiveness and its exactitude of phrase and image, a deeply restless and troubled novel, a novel which exchanges youthful exuberance for disorientation and despair and which seems unwilling or unable to establish narrative momentum on its own terms. Perhaps slightly idiosyncratically, and certainly in opposition to that perceptible ripple of current critical opinion which mourns the loss in *NW* of the rhetorical ease and verbal fluency of Smith's previous fiction, it seems to me that the gathering agitation and unevenness of her prose is an interesting and potentially enriching development that might presage a vital and vitalising new phase in her writing. I say this as one of those readers whom, while marvelling at the narrative poise, self-confidence and circumambient dexterity of her debut *White Teeth,* saw in her almost preternatural ability to reproduce and ventriloquise the surface styles, brandings and registers of public culture a fateful gift that might culminate in either a pseudo-ironic trafficking in cliché and opinion or the well-meaning (but also vaguely self-pleasuring) circulation of *bien-pensant* axioms and attitudes. Despite its substantial faults and weakness (and the book is in some ways, not least structurally, a mess and a failure), *NW* is an *interesting* novel, a novel that shows a writer thinking, adjusting herself, rethinking her subject, trying to get at what it is in her subject that agitates and absorbs her, trying to get it *right*. And it is, to cut to the chase a little, worth reading on those terms alone.

It's revealing when thinking about *NW* to consider how little of the novel's interest resides in plot details. It is true, of course, that in a certain sense the novel is 'about' a long friendship between two 30-something women who both grew up on the Caldwell Estate in Willesden: Leah Hanwell, a 'white' (Anglo-Irish) sometime philosophy graduate who now works for a non-profit organisation and whose Franco-African partner Michel spends his spare time trying sedulously to improve their social standing by becoming a trader in internet shares, and the 'black' (West-Indian diaspora) Natalie (*née* Keisha) Blake, an upwardly mobile young barrister fresh from Cambridge University and an English Literature degree. Both of these women will experience a crisis in their relationship to their backgrounds and each other; both will be visited by terrifying bouts of self-abandonment and despair. But if the principal concern of the novel lies in unfolding the parallel, diverging and interrelated stories of Leah and Natalie (for childhood Kiesha is now Natalie, self-invention progressively occupying the very centre of who she is), this concern is leavened and enriched by the imaginative presence of both Felix Cooper, a young black film-maker and former drug-dealer trying to turn his life around (and whose childhood and adolescence in the subaltern Garvey House Estate provides lingering memories of the struggle carried out by the 1970s immigrant West Indian community for rights and recognition), and the spectral figure of Nathan Bogle, Leah and Natalie's childhood friend, whose immiserated involvement in drug culture and street crime offers a sobering reminder of the fate reserved for the underclass in the modern metropolis.

The text of *NW* is divided into five sections or movements (for Smith, like her great modernist predecessors, thinks as much in terms of the musical cadence and phrase as she does in linear narrative sequences) entitled 'Visitation', 'Guest', 'Host' and 'Crossing' before concluding once more in 'Visitation'. Each of these sections explores the situation, mood and temperament of one of its three principal characters (for Nathan remains a marginal, although brooding, presence, throughout the novel while Smith shows little interest in stimulating our interest in Michel or Frank, Natalie's husband, beyond the basic plot developments they make possible). The novel begins with a violent and wholly unexpected intrusion into domesticity from the outside world – a young, manipulative woman imposes upon Leah in her home, crafts a tale of abjection designed to solicit both Leah's sympathy and her cash, leaving her feeling simultaneously exploited and ashamed – and much of its fascination for us lies in the way it shows its characters exposed to a sense of contingency they never imagined possible, a confrontation with raw circumstance through which they glimpse the fragility or fraudulence of the stories they have told themselves about who they are, where they come from, and where they might be going, and the need to fashion a new way of being that might once more make their lives valuable to themselves. One of the key weaknesses of the novel, however, is that

Leah Hanwell is not really interesting enough as a character to animate the acres of narrative space lavished upon her moods and movements, and Smith struggles to fashion a style distinctive enough to capture the rhythms of her fluctuating engagement with and recoil from the world, employing her rather too obviously as a surrogate narrator upon the author's own behalf. It is a different story with Felix Cooper, the central protagonist of 'Ghost', whose tentative attempts to find some measure of autonomy and independence are rendered with a degree of poise, pathos and delicacy of touch and execution the equal of anything Smith has ever written. Both Felix's essential benignity of nature and his emerging fixity of purpose are superbly realised in two extended set-piece exchanges (one with a former girl-friend and drug partner, the other with a minor scion of the metropolitan monied elite), and it is a pity in every sense that his presence in the novel is cruelly curtailed. But the lasting achievement of *NW* is to be found in the character of Natalie/Keisha Blake, who is at once the most provoking and enigmatic of all of Smith's fictional creations. The story of Natalie's desperate ('traumatised' might not be too strong a word) struggle to escape the economic and racial confines of the Caldwell Estate, reinvent her own origins and achieve the security and freedom of upper middle-class professional life is both a triumph and a tragedy that seems to destroy the ground of her own personality and leave her with no permanent sense of belonging and no fixed emotional or social abode. Some of the novel's late scenes, indeed, in which Natalie, now perhaps reverting back to Keisha, embarks on a nomadic tour of her London past with the bemused Nathan Bogle in tow, possess a strange and uncanny power that continues to haunt the imagination long after the text's other details have begun to fade from view.

If *NW* is not always a successful or wholly convincing piece of writing – it dispenses too abruptly with absorbing characters, fails sufficiently to vivify one of its two central protagonists, and relies too heavily upon a number of plot devices, such as Natalie's sudden predilection for random internet-generated sexual hook-ups, which seem bathetic and contrived – it also offers an intriguing clue about Zadie Smith's future novelistic direction. One of the signal achievements of her work over the last decade or so lies in its dramatisation of the various ways her characters have sought to develop a shared sense of belonging, community and ethics from those things they hold in common: childhood memories, inherited traditions, ways of speaking, scraps of popular culture, or fabricated and reinvented histories. What Smith gives us in the erratic and anomic figure of Natalie/Keisha Blake, however, is a character who experiences the rich possibilities of reciprocity and mutuality as forms of fraudulence and abjection and who can only glimpse the image of her own possible freedom in the destitution, not the restitution, of shared dreams and longings. Such a character pushes Smith beyond the generic norms of Forsterian irony or the multicultural comedy of manners towards an implicitly tragic cast of mind. It is an artistic trajectory paradoxically full of hope and promise, not least because it promises to pay considerable imaginative dividends in the years ahead.

Lee Spinks

Love's Bonfire. Faber & Faber. ISBN 9780571271535. £12.99
Tom Paulin

This is a book full of all kinds of dwelling places in various states of repair: domestic, civic, agricultural, temporary, at sea. By the end of the volume, 'the Atlantic world' is compared to a 'massy cruise ship floating nine / stories high near some rutputty Roman port' ('The Choice'). Old family houses are re-made in memory, bungalows blight the Donegal skyline, walls and dividing places in Walid Khazendhar's Palestine are broken through, cracked, disturbed, and then disappear. When we do get 'home' in the poems, it's ripe for takeover. At one stage, in 'No Packdrill', there is no less than a stranger in the house, from whose 'shaving tackle' the poet recoils:

> I should call him Roger
> though he wasn't that
> a canny dope
> an early jogger
> reminding me that objects
> which are both ugly and utile
> often leave you feeling slightly soiled.

That sense of being soiled is matched by thinking things you really shouldn't in words you shouldn't really use. Not just his 'tackle' but Roger's razor is 'a bit brassy bit genital'. A husband's desire to 'slash the badger' comes only too true as an actual badger is run over by the poet's car. All thoughts of love are lost in recoil after roadkill is followed by body parts on the TV in an Irish bar. Home ends up invaded by lodgers, or traded for a B&B, and one dominant feeling in this book is guilt and self-loathing, where innuendo becomes middle-aged dis-ease. 'No Packdrill' ends up with impotence after the innuendo:

> – I reach out now what
> six seventeen years later?
> reach out to collect
> my own tackle
> from the glass shelf
> in a hotel bathroom

and see a version of myself
touched by fear and guilt
like a face at a window

So *Love's Bonfire* isn't exactly a barrel of laughs. It is a collection of aftermath and indirection, seeking dwelling places and locations at once homely and *unheimlich*, shot through with the allegiances of family and politics now turned to insecurity, uncertainty, fear and guilt.

Paulin's poems typically inhabit a Northern February: weak-lit, jerry-built, like a memory of long-gone Du Barry's bar in the Belfast docks, 'damp rackety packed with seamen dockers rentboys hoors'. Paulin's deliberately rackety lexis spells out a Northern vernacular (English and Irish) which has always spoken of commitment to the ramshackle, the marginal or the misunderstood. The controversy which has followed him meant that critics have seen this breezeblock quality as bogus, at odds with the political preoccupations of a poet and critic who ventured big views on big topics to big audiences who listened to him because he was good value. The goodness of that value seems to have seeped away in this book, and the danger is of a slide into self-pity, even sentimentality. But the sense of vulnerability that brings with it means the shrugging off of the vatic and dogmatic throughout. The civic intellectual finds himself marginalised in civic space just as domestic spaces crumble.

Being Paulin, the poems are filled full of allusions to others' works – and the central section is entirely made up of versions of Khazender in which middle-eastern sun and flowers peek, albeit through broken buildings. Old Field Day flames flicker from time to time, particularly Seamus Heaney's preoccupation with voice and place: in 'And No More Be Seen' the word *'throughother'* is reclaimed from Heaney and W.R. Rodgers. The poem also remembers Tony Harrison's Wordsworth from 'Them and [uz]', as it recalibrates 'water' into 'watter' in order to rhyme with 'matter'. Reclaiming domestic as much as linguistic space involves a symbolic wiping clean of a green oilcloth and the colour green reappears in 'Same Ould Strop'. That poem revisits the *dinnseanchas* (lore of place name) poem, with a hint at the position statement in Heaney's conversation with schoolfriend Seamus Deane in 'Ministry of Fear' in *North*: 'Ulster was British but with no rights / on the English lyric'. Paulin substitutes an unknowingness, a place which cannot be a property:

But mind you've no rights
– no rights of knowledge

no rights of property
on that clanky sound *dinnseanchas*
they're hard nuts these placenames
– why crack them again?
or they're bolts you can't force

This notion of being unable to gain forced entry into lore of place is reassuring in 'Same Ould Strop'. But dispossession is everywhere in the book. In the versions of Khazendar, dwelling place and imaginative space are worked together with a light sprinkling of Heidegger. 'Being in Time' we discover, is about a being a bee in time. Possession over doors, thresholds and lintels is revealed as lost, imaged from an abandoned toybox as presage of the loss of self: 'our keys were like plasticine / and our shadows melted in the sunset'. 'Starting from Scratch' tells a more obvious historical allegory of the invention of post-war Palestine: 'Mesopotamia / its borders redrawn one countryhouse weekend / in a not quite island called England'. But then 'The Sail, Again' sees uprooting as a new direction, the cracked plaster block-built house with a picture of a sail on the wall as a symbol of partial deliverance: 'sure it was torn to bits / but still it led the wind'.

The loosely-gathered initial sequence around the title poem brings together personal loss and the destruction of buildings, dwellings and thinking about them. 'Love's bonfire' is the *veteris vestigiae flammae,* the embers of an old flame which haunt these poems of courtship and married life followed by divorce and 'permanent pain'. None of the poems are in the business of blame, but they can be painfully first-person and at times they break out of their allusiveness in a confessional mode that we do not necessarily associate with the magpie modernism of Paulin the recycler of the dissenting voices of Mandelstam or Hazlitt or Milton. The models here are the oblique love poems of Lowell or Bishop, and the love's bonfire motif is taken from Hardy's *Poems of 1912–1913*, and in particular his poem of utter change, 'Where the Picnic Was'. That poem, like these, needless to say, was no picnic, and where in Hardy the death of his wife followed a divided married life, here in Paulin a darkened self seeks form after breakdown. It is poetry of the life-change, uncertainty before worlds which have somehow been rebuilt and have re-emerged into weak light in unrecognisable shapes. Paulin forsakes the Dickinsonian dashes and question marks which are the only marks of punctuation in the rest of the volume for rare full-stops in these poems. He gives up the illusion of untrammelled syntactic flow for grammatical division.

At times the syntax sorts disarming memories in seemingly artless ways:

> I saw then I recall
> that we were quite different people
> – you were active
> didn't want the arranged marriage
> and believed we had a future
> while I feared that it—the marriage
> would happen for definite
> and saw your mother weeping your father mad and angry
> the tough cousins massing
> you saying no this can never be Tom
> and me saying wanly
> Giti I love you so dearly
> and I will for always
> but I can see you can't bring shame
> down on your family your tribe.

There is a vulnerable, not quiet articulated pain in these poems, memories of a life lived together in various homes, or even just overnight stays, which are remembered in the addresses and place names over which the *dinnseanchas* exercises no rights.

One poem tries to put things back together again, trading Heidegger and Derek Mahon for a declaration of things in space. 'Shades Off, No Sheds' is about corrugated iron buildings crowding up to a hilltop farmhouse, and echoes Mahon's great poem about absence and history, 'A Disused Shed in County Wexford'. Paulin attempts a Thomist rewrite, swapping the Mahon stanza for a seemingly loose but nevertheless highly structured piece of rhyming. The poem then attempts to piece together broken and purposeless remnants into meaning:

> so I imagine turning the earth
> and finding bits of broken delph
> and those shards marking
> what somewhere is called *the real presence*
> – break a cup a bowl a plate

a beer whiskey or lemonade bottle
then chuck their fragments – brish –
chuck those bits of hard brittle eggshell
straight in the midden
like casualties after some battle
– can we say then that such an action begins
whatever it is those sheds those barns
are trying hard to block out?

If the word 'block' in its various meanings inhabits many of these poems, the recycling of fire in a midden seems to be one way of breaking the block. Obscured space is shoved up against the house, seeking shape and form. Whether '*the real presence*' can be reconstructed and remnants of self and home rebuilt is perhaps rhetorical; but the question is good, if unanswerable.

Forsaking the 'daylight gods' in 'The Choice', the poet ends on another side in a process of re-formation, part Adam in Genesis, part shade in Hades:

– here it's dark downward without form
as I drop through it spineless a hugger of shadows
like a criminal or an agent – look at me soaked
in some foreign port some dockside dive
where I could if I wanted add spit to the sawdust
and feel maybe a shade better

This is the mode of many of the poems: a soak in a dive, the small consolation of the pun. As the penultimate poem in the collection, the equivocal optimism of its last words, 'a shade better', cannot offer a final word.

The book's last lyric is 'Shy Willows' which offers a vision of swallows in flight, 'sewing nothing with nothing'. Yeats touches the poem as it puns its way from swallow to sallows to sallies to Gardens, but Paulin's bête noire, Eliot, is here as well, on Margate sands connecting nothing with nothing. *Love's Bonfire* ends up holding out on the verge of nothingness, the poet imagining 'river gardens' against city buildings, sorting out true and false etymologies.

Matthew Campbell

The Heart Broke In. Canongate. ISBN 9780857862907. £17.99
James Meek

Ritchie Shepherd, erstwhile rock star, now hosts a TV show *Teen Makeover* and lives comfortably with his wife Karin (co-star in the rock band) and their children. He has a lifestyle many would envy, yet he jeopardises everything by having an affair with one of the show's 15-year-old participants: 'He'd discovered that he felt no shame about cheating on Karin until she found out'. It isn't his wife but the girl's mother who finds out, and Ritchie's situation becomes a trap he has to extricate himself from. His sister Bec is a malaria researcher on the verge of a breakthrough. When she jilts her fiancé, Val, a powerful newspaper editor and founder of the Moral Foundation, his sense of grievance leads him to uncover Ritchie's indiscretion and threaten him with exposure – unless Ritchie can find a better story about someone close to him. As it happens, Bec hooks up with Alex, Ritchie's former drummer, who also happens to be a genius of Molecular Biology, and the two become a celebrated science couple in the media, he fronting a TV show and she championing a new treatment to prevent malaria. When she in turn commits an indiscretion, Ritchie is faced with the dilemma of whether to dish the dirt on his sister to Val and the Moral Foundation to save his own skin, or lose everything he has worked for – celebrity status, house, family, income – and be sent to prison for good measure.

Reprobate Ritchie is hardly a sympathetic protagonist, yet he is complicated by a deep longing to prove himself 'a good man', and to some extent comes close when he finds it within himself to forgive his soldier father's murderer, an IRA member now turned poet. Even here his forgiveness is somewhat tainted by a less altruistic drive to make a film of their meeting, and it is Bec who forgives him in a way that is truly redeeming and leads to closure for her. However, it is a measure of Meek's skill that we come to feel empathy if not sympathy with the scurrilous Ritchie. He is put through a relentless moral mincer, and we relish the mental anguish he brings on himself because it is no more than he deserves, but he has a certain Dostoevskian self-awareness which makes him a worthy player in a moral thriller such as this. Though he exasperates us by being foolish, selfish, narcissistic and disloyal by turns, we are made to feel the intense discomfort of the moral corner Meek forces him into.

Meek's main thematic territory is loyalty and betrayal, and the Moral Foundation is a convenient device to have his characters betraying each other all over the place. The plot is a good deal more complex than I have made it sound, involving many surprising reversals and sub-plots. Perhaps it has to be to sustain interest in a novel of this length, though it could be argued that the narrative impact is rather diluted by the sprawling nature of this family saga and might have been tauter at two-thirds of the length. At times the moral concerns underpinning the action are teased out in dialogue to the point of becoming explicit, as in a confrontation scene between Ritchie and Bec:

'You're such a coward.'

'I nearly died!' shouted Ritchie. 'I hung myself. I only just managed to get my head out of the noose. It was your fault. You made me feel worthless. You made me feel that I wasn't a good man.'

Bec squatted down close to Ritchie and said softly: 'Maybe you're not a good man. Maybe you're a bad man. Have you considered that?'

However, *The Heart Broke In* is never less than readable and there are some wonderfully comic scenes. In a way it reads like a nineteenth-century novel, although the characters are moving in a very modern world of *Teen Makeover* and gene therapy, and I am sure this is quite deliberate. It is certainly replete with colourful, if sometimes rather improbable characters (notably the molecular-biologist-drummer) who lead eventful lives, and it does nothing if not address some of the moral concerns of our times – child exploitation and abuse, blackmail, privacy and the press, and the ethics of torture.

Brian McCabe

Happy Hour. Gallery Press. ISBN 9781852355333. £10.50
Andrew Jamison

Sad and wonderful tension between what is sublime and what is commonplace – an astonishment at this world, augmented by the sardonic awareness that astonishment is nothing new – permeates themes of transience in Andrew Jamison' first collection, *Happy Hour.*

Critics may find some of these poems hackneyed, but I believe the poet is up to something. 'The Bus to Belfast' opens in the voice of a pre-transient speaker. The eponymous bus and its 'pane's black rubber seal... nicked to bits / by a penknife' are as drab a welcome as any; however, in its first line, a sleight of hand evokes a dual theme of loss and scrutiny.

> An unstubbed cigarette butt – I can picture it now –

Jamison isolates the image in the midst of its disappearance. He does not witness a total burn-out 'smouldering at the door of Toal's', but imagines what once was visible. Such nostalgia informs 'The Curzon' as well, where the speaker remembers the darkness of a cinema visit, how 'seats are taken, lights dimmed, minds blown.' The poem opens with the daring conjunction 'And' (à la Heaney's 'St. Kevin and the Blackbird') to establish a tense narrative that carries the book.

In fact, it would be easy to overlook how the collection is interwoven. 'The Curzon' with its haunting 'And there we are:' devolves into solitude in the following poem 'Listening to Ash' ('And there I am'). These rhetorical parallels dart in and out of *Happy Hour.* Likewise, 'Listening to Ash' is only the first of a series of poems about listening to bands (Them and Kings of Convenience also get their mentions). For this speaker music is one more impetus for nostalgia, a feature of evanescent relationships. With it's common themes connecting them, the poems fly together, reinforcing such loneliness 'as I begrudge the moment its prerogative / to come and go, to up and leave' ('Summer's Time').

Tension mounts in Jamison's versions of Jorge Guillen, Manuel Bandeira and Pablo Neruda. This draw to Spanish and Portuguese poetry interprets the seemingly-banal features of other poems. For example, 'Killyleagh Road at Night in Snow' (after Neruda) targets a lack of fulfillment in terms of time.

> This should be the hour of fallen leaves
> but is instead the hour of fallen snow.
> I ponder old predicaments:

when there are words there seldom is a pen;
when there's a pen the words are seldom there.

Such 'old predicaments', as Jamison hazards, extend his scope from poetic versions to mythology. Aristotle has 'quite a lot to say for himself' in 'London'; Orpheus is asked to 'play us out' (though the speaker 'can't be sure about all this'); and 'Baucis and Philemon' are retold in a memorial to grandparents.

Further afield, *Happy Hour* dips in and out of America via New York City. If Jamison is tuned to any American voices, his ear inclines somewhere between Frost and O'Hara. 'What I'll Say When I Get Back' claims 'This is the place, I'll say, no one and nothing/ but a two-seat bench I'll sit on by myself'. The pastoral scene is propped up with 'sheep shit and rocks/ and puddles and muck which will take' the walking speaker home. However, he does not arrive home, and the poem turns on an 'if'. This meditative 'if' is how we 'see the path goes on and *is* the path' (emphasis added). It is the crafted ambivalence of 'is' to which I keep returning. 'If' posits indecision, and 'is' suggests, but does not define, some truth about that path and *not* taking it. Of course, a path is another symbol of transience, and indecision is reinforced (following a stoic enjambment) by the word 'might'.

But if I'll hold on
I'll see the path goes on and is the path
I might yet take, leading as it does

After this pastoral episode, Jamison meditates on 'the all-encompassing silence of ourselves' in 'At the End of the Day', 'When all the cups of tea are drunk, dinners done' and 'we, loud-mouthed, return/ to our respective rooms'. Separation by rooms makes home 'where we practice solitude', likewise, separate from 'the constant imposition of sky and grass'.

In the end, readers of *Happy Hour* may feel caught between the commonplace and the timeless, haunted by a growing sense that 'There's bound to be something in this' ('Autumning'). At the same time they may feel like Jamison's starlings in 'The Starlings', 'tremendously alike, / tremendously alone'. They will be right, of course. But by my lights, these poems evoke the loneliness of an imagination caught between its rural and urban predilections. These are musings on moving forward, but often do not arrive anywhere. Still, it is easy to imagine the poet winking after all of this. These poems are also about buses.

Andrew D. Eaton

The Oak and the Ash and the Wild Cherry Tree. Gallery Press. ISBN 9781852355340. £10.50
Kerry Hardie

Kerry Hardie's newest collection is a dark and gorgeous hymn to human mortality. Death is, of course, such a common theme in poetry that it's difficult to find anything new to say about it, but Hardie succeeds, injecting into these poems her usual quiet originality. For her, death is not to be feared – if anything, it is a place of comfort and safety. The refrain of 'Sixty', the first poem in the collection, is 'everyone is slowly going home,' and elsewhere, in the afterlife of 'The Inmost Sea', the dead 'stretch in the fresh red graves / fennel and dill line the breath of the wind.' Life, Hardie reckons, is messy – in 'Happy Endings', a scene of children playing on the beach becomes a metaphor for the way things inevitably unravel.

> There was a plan, but it went with the tide;
> everyone ended up too drunk to stand,
> our shoes floated off and we grizzled with cold
> and the evening light pearled the wavering line
> where the sea took the edge off the land.

Death, meanwhile, brings clarity. In the final stanza of 'Timing', the speaker hears of the death of her neighbour, and like the spring that has just arrived, the news allows her to see the world afresh.

> When the death news ran we looked at the ground
> where our feet were planted. Then off somewhere.
> Between two trees.
> At the patched door on a stone shed.
> At the post van, disappearing.

Death in Hardie's poems is a release from the process she finds truly terrifying: the slow decay of ageing. Old age, she says in 'Sixty', 'is not how I want things to be. / It cancels the contract of life, / it stifles our birth-howl.' In the collection's title poem, the speaker's mother is eerily transformed into a tree: 'she is old now. She sways / though no wind blows.' And in 'Waning', Hardie laments, 'all that I love is alive and already dying.'

> How can we love
> when love must watch life cease to live?

> How can we not
> when downy seeds blow the ripe roads?

In previous collections, Hardie has written a great deal about death in nature: the triumph of summer and the inevitable descent into winter. So it is no wonder that this collection, although more heavily populated by humans, also tips its hat to the beauty and cruelty of nature. 'October', another extended metaphor for ageing and death, illustrates the way in which the movement of the seasons ruthlessly changes the natural landscape.

> But the golden goose will drown in the night
> of the deep black rains of November.
> The little red fox will shrivel and starve,
> his white bones will lie in the fields.

In 'How We Carry On Pretending', the ageing woman becomes an overgrown house: the idea of death as a way of 'returning to nature' taken literally.

> Instead, there is a small, tired house,
> half derelict, and anyone can see
> the forked crack gaping in the gable end,
> the ivy pushing from inside the rooms,
> levering its way through the empty frames,
> reaching its scabby arms towards the light.

In the natural world Hardie inhabits, humans are always insignificant, vulnerable. But hers are not the dwarfed humans of the sublime experience: these poems are not about awesome mountains or breath-taking vistas. Hardie takes a more ecological approach: in these poems, humans are merely another kind of animal living inside and alongside nature.

> Away in the distance the pup was clearing the gulls
> Right under my feet the suck of watery sands,
> the ooze and wormcasts squirming between my toes.
>
> I was a dot, a tiny concentration
> of blood and bone and intelligence
> moving about
> under all that vastness.

In 'Fruit Net', the speaker holds a trapped bird she has freed, and feels her own kinship with another creature. 'It stills, I still. It rests within my hands, / its life as intense as mine.' And in 'From Time to Time Red Dog Shows Up in the Forest', the speaker greets a strange dog, animal to animal, and realises her own insignificance.

> Great cauliflower-domed seed heads of hogweed
> tower the overgrown path.
> Then he's off.
> Dogness of dog
> into woodness of woods.
> My feet make small sounds in the silence.

The feeling that runs throughout the collection is that of time running out: seasons changing, the familiar disappearing, death approaching ever faster. This shows not just in the content, but in the poems' sparseness, too. In comparison to her previous collections, the lines here are shorter, the poems barer and more urgent. Hardie dedicates the collection to her brother, who died, she adds, at forty-seven. In 'The Emigrant's Photo', she describes the photographed man as 'warm and alive with death.' This is also a fitting description for a book of poems that celebrates the wonder of our small lives as much as it laments their brevity.

Claire Askew

Cold Sea Stories. Comma Press. ISBN 9781905583393. £7.99
Pawel Huelle

The Polish writer Pawel Huelle likes his books to talk to other books, to reference other books, to engage in a dialogue with them. If this sounds overly worthy and intellectual, I can vouch for the fact that this isn't the case. His 2005 book *Mercedes-Benz* – variously described as a novel and a memoir – in which the great Czech writer, Bohumil Hrabal, is addressed throughout, is highly enjoyable and inclusively clever (if possibly bemusing for anyone unfamiliar with Hrabal's work).

That of course, may be an issue. When I read Huelle's first novel *Who is David Weiser?* – some years ago now, I didn't make the connection between it and the work of Gunter Grass, though probably I should have. I enjoyed the novel but must have lost something. That I'm also reading Huelle in translation suggests that I have lost even more; reading a work in translation, you inevitably lose something of the poetry of the original language. Perhaps all writing is a translation of sorts, a conquering of the obstacles of communication, a translation of the writer's thoughts into words, a transformation from uncensored emotions and untidy ideas to the crafted, directed 'translated' text. If you're wondering why I mention poetry, I go along with the Irish fiction writer John McGahern who says: 'There's verse and there's prose and then there's poetry, and poetry can happen in either.'

In the afterword to *Cold Sea Stories*, Huelle says: 'I wrote them around the age of fifty, in the realisation that I am a man of the Baltic… This is the culture of herrings, potatoes and vodka, not wine, and this is the place that has shaped me, like it or not.' Huelle talks a great deal about the history of the area but doesn't restrict his cultural obsessions to national boundaries. Thematically and geographically, these are wide-ranging stories with surprisingly little vodka or potatoes in them. Taking his cue from Borges, Huelle perceives his identity as much in terms of his reading as that of his everyday existence; books are yet again at the centre of most of these stories, whether it be the bible, the I Ching, or a toy catalogue.

These are often unashamedly complex narratives, which move between time zones, between straightforward storytelling and metanarrative ('Mimesis'), between autobiography and invention, ('The Bicycle Express'), where Huelle draws on his own youthful involvement with Solidarnosc, between love story and farce ('Franz Carl Weber') – between realism and the fantastical, as in 'Ukiel', in which Sir Henry Raeburn's famous skating minister makes a cameo reappearance on a frozen Polish lake, and one which has an old Prussian name, a name from a vanished people. 'The Fifteen Glasses of Gendarme Polanke' with its echoes of Chekhov, is not only an impressive handling of simultaneous action – so difficult to pull off – but a clear-eyed and vivid critique of state authority. The premise of the story is simple enough – while Polanke props up the bar and indulges in ludicrous delusions of grandeur, an affecting human story is happening beyond his narrow vision.

With its echoes of Borges, there is the seductively elusive allegory, 'Abulafia':

> In the desert, at an oasis also called No, there were supposed to be three standing stones with inscriptions. No one had seen them, but Pliny and Herodotus wrote about them. These inscriptions contained the universal patterns for all alphabets and languages ...

Language, in particular lost language – and with it lost culture – is an abiding preoccupation and always carries a political or emotive charge:

> She [his mother] took her greatest secret with her: the language she had never passed on to him, which would always bring him the scent of haymaking, clover, a wind from the sea and clouds.' (Abulafia)

This preoccupation is not surprising from a writer whose national boundaries have altered so dramatically. Another Polish writer, Olga Tokarczuk once told me: My country is my language. A small gripe: it may be a translation or editorial issue but clichés like 'what riveted his attention' 'he couldn't tear his eyes away from' 'his gaze and attention were entirely riveted' really don't do this work any service, though it could be said that riveting does have a special resonance with Solidarnosc.

One of the underlying themes which runs through the collection is the link between historical and present day wonders, romances and atrocities. Huelle has spoken of his fondness for the circular narrative and there is a sense of circularity in this collection; a motif introduced in the opening story resurfaces in the final piece. The story world depicted in *Cold Sea Stories*, feels too impressively sprawling, too convincingly messy – like life – to benefit from this tidiness.

Dilys Rose

Notes on Contributors

Gary Allen is an award-winning poet from Nr. Ireland. Widely published in international magazines including, *Agenda, Ambit, Antigonish Review, Dark Horse, Fiddlehead, Irish Pages, London Magazine, Malahat Review, Meanjin, Poetry Ireland,* the *Poetry Review, Stand,* the *Threepenney Review,* the *Yellow Nib,* etc. A twelfth collection, *Mexico,* will be published early 2013 by Agenda Editions. A selecton of his poetry was published in the anthology, *The New North,* Wake Forest University Press, North Carolina and in the UK by Salt Publishing.

Simon Armitage lives in West Yorkshire and is Professor of Poetry at the University of Sheffield. His most recent publications are *Seeing Stars* (Faber, 2010) and *The Death of King Arthur* (Faber 2011), a medieval translation in the style of his acclaimed *Sir Gawain and the Green Knight. Walking Home* (Faber 2012), a prose account of his troubadour journey along the Pennine Way, was a *Sunday Times* Best-Seller. He is also a novelist and broadcaster and writes extensively for radio and television. His two latest plays are *Black Roses: the Killing of Sophie Lancaster* (BBC Radio 4/Manchester Royal Exchange) and *The Torch Bearers* (BBC Radio 3/The Baltic).

Claire Askew is a writer and educator from Edinburgh. Her reviews and non-fiction have appeared in the *Scottish Review of Books, The Skinny* and *xoJane,* and her poetry has been published in the *Guardian, Popshot, PANK,* and elsewhere. She works as a further education lecturer at Edinburgh College, teaching Literature and Communication.

Kevin Cahill was born in Cork City, Ireland, in 1975, where he still lives. He is currently working towards a first collection of poetry and to date his work has appeared in journals such as the *London Magazine, Berkeley Poetry Review, Magma, Poetry Ireland Review, Agenda, Envoi, Crannóg,* and *The SHOp.*

Ian Campbell retired in 2009 from the English Department at the University of Edinburgh, where he is Emeritus Professor of Scottish and Victorian Literature, and teaching fellow. He has worked since 1964 on *The Collected Letters of Thomas and Jane Welsh Carlyle,* of which he is now one of the senior editors, and has published widely on Victorian and Scottish topics.

Matthew Campbell teaches English at the University of York. He is the author of books and articles on Irish and Victorian poetry and is currently writing a history of modern Irish poetry.

Michael Cronin teaches translation in Dublin City University. He is Editor of the New Perspectives in Translation Series at Routledge and Chairperson of Poetry Ireland.

Paul Crosthwaite is a Lecturer in the Department of English Literature at the University of Edinburgh. He has published widely on modern literature, and is currently completing a book about contemporary culture and financial markets.

Andrew Eaton is an American poet living in Belfast. He is an Editorial Assistant at *Irish Pages* and a PhD student at the Seamus Heaney Centre for Poetry. His poems are published in *Magma* and *14 Magazine*.

Jen Hadfield has published two collections of poetry with Bloodaxe Books: *Almanacs* (2005) and *Nigh-No-Place* which won the T.S. Eliot Prize in 2008. She lives in Shetland and blogs intermittently at rogueseeds.blogpsot.com.

Sally Hinchcliffe was born in London and grew up all over the world, finally settling near Dumfries. Her first novel, *Out Of a Clear Sky*, was published by Pan Macmillan in 2008 and became a Radio 4 Book at Bedtime.

Daniel Jewesbury is an artist and writer. He has been a co-editor of *Variant* magazine for over a decade, and is currently working on a new film portrait of Belfast filmed entirely in its cemeteries and burial grounds.

Stuart Kelly is a literary critic and writes regularly for the *Scotsman*, *Scotland on Sunday*, the *Guardian* and *The Times*. He is the author of *The Book of Lost Books* and *Scott-Land: The Man Who Invented a Nation*, which was longlisted for the Samuel Johnson Prize and was BBC Radio 4's Book of the Week.

Thomas Legendre is the author of *The Burning* and several short stories, the most recent of which appeared in *4'33" Audio Magazine*. He has also written the play *Half Life*, performed as part of NVA's art installation in conjunction with the National Theatre of Scotland, and a radio drama, *Dream Repair,* broadcast on BBC 4. He is a Lecturer in Creative Writing at the University of Nottingham.

Frances Leviston's first collection, *Public Dream*, was published in 2007 and shortlisted for the T S Eliot Prize. Her poems have appeared in the *LRB*, the *Guardian*, *The Times*, and the *TLS*. She works as a freelance reviewer and poetry tutor.

Brian McCabe has published three collections of poetry, the most recent being *Zero* (Polygon, 2009). He has published one novel and five collections of short stories, the most recent being *A Date With My Wife* (Canongate, 2001). His *Selected Stories* was published by Argyll in 2003.

Hannah McGill is mostly a film critic, and from 2006 to 2010 was Artistic Director of the Edinburgh International Film Festival. Her fiction writing has appeared in a number of collections and been broadcast on BBC Radio 4. She lives in Edinburgh.

Willy Maley is Professor of English Literature at Glasgow University. In 1995 he co-founded with Philip Hobsbaum the Creative Writing programme there. His recent work includes *Muriel Spark for Starters* (Capercaillie, 2008), and, as co-editor with Michael Gardiner, *The Edinburgh Companion to Muriel Spark* (Edinburgh University Press, 2010).

Conor O'Callaghan is from Dundalk, lives in Manchester and teaches in both Sheffield Hallam and Lancaster. A fourth collection of poems, *Swell* (Gallery Press), is due in spring 2013.

Jacob Polley's third book of poems, *The Havocs*, is short-listed for this year's T.S. Eliot Prize. His novel, *Talk of the Town*, won the 2010 Somerset Maugham Award. Jacob lives in Fife and teaches at the University of St Andrews.

Dilys Rose has published ten books of fiction and poetry, including *Red Tides*, *Pest Maiden*, *War Dolls* and *Bodywork*. She is programme director of the MSc in Creative Writing by online learning at the University of Edinburgh.

Anne Rouse was born in Washington DC, grew up in Virginia and now lives in Hastings. She has published four collections: *Sunset Grill* (1993), *Timing* (1997) – both Poetry Book Society Recommendations – *The School of Night* (2004); and *The Upshot: New & Selected Poems* (2008) all published by Bloodaxe.

Lee Spinks teaches in the English Department of Edinburgh University and is currently writing a study of Norman Mailer.

Will Stone is a poet, essayist and literary translator. His first collection, *Glaciation* (Salt, 2007), won the international Glen Dimplex Award for poetry (2008). His second, *Drawing in Ash* (Salt, 2011) won the *3am magazine* book of the year award.

Dawn Wood grew up in Omagh, Co. Tyrone, and now lives in Perthshire, working as a science lecturer at the University of Abertay, Dundee. She has published *Quarry* (Templar Poetry, 2008), *Connoisseur* (2009) and *Hermes with Gift* (UAD Press, 2011).

How to Subscribe to Edinburgh Review

Individual subscriptions (3 issues annually) £20 within the UK; £28 abroad.

Institutional subscriptions (3 issues annually) £35 within the UK; £43 abroad.

You can subscribe online at www.edinburgh-review.com
or send a cheque to

Edinburgh Review
22a Buccleuch Place
Edinburgh EH8 9LN

Most back issues are available at £7.99 each.

You'll find the *Edinburgh Review* website at

http://www.edinburgh-review.com

Please join us on Facebook and Twitter.